CW00524142

THE SHORT STORY

OF A

LONG LIFE

by

P. E. Leatham

Published in Great Britain
by
WILTON 65
Hernes Keep, Winkfield, Windsor, Berkshire SL4 4SY
2009

ISBN 978-1-905060-14-6

My thanks go to my son, Simon, for his enthusiastic encouragement and for introducing me to Sarah McQuillen, who has faithfully transcribed my ramblings!

To Elizabeth

With best wishes.

Patricia Highsmith

I was born in London in 1925.

I was a big disappointment to my mother, who was so sure that I was a boy, she had been calling me 'Edward' for nine months and, after my arrival, took a considerable amount of time to find an alternative name.

She was very ill at the time of my birth and was subsequently told that she could have no more children. This was a big blow to her, and an even bigger blow to my American grandmother, Betty Beauchamp. Her husband Edward had been honoured with a Baronetcy and, if there were no more boys in the family, the title would die with my father.

We lived in a very small house in a place called Deanery Street, which ran parallel with what is now the Dorchester Hotel. In those days, it was a very grand private residence called Dorchester House. My first recollection is of looking out of my nursery window into the windows opposite and seeing the footmen in their white powdered wigs and braided uniforms going to and fro, carrying large plates of food to the dining room.

Fairly shortly, we moved to a larger house, near my grandmother's home in Grosvenor Place.

I was very fond of my paternal grandmother and spent a lot of time with her as a child. She lived by herself, as her husband was much older than her and had died before I was born.

Betty had two children – Edward, who was killed in the 1914–18 war, and my father, Brograve, known as Bro for short. We often wondered where the name came from until, one day, I was reading a book about Norfolk. Apparently, the Brograves are the dry land between the sea and the Broads.

Little Brograve was lucky to survive. His nanny decided to take him out for a walk in his pram one day. All of a sudden, a horse dragging a Royal Mail van bolted, heading straight for the pram. A passer-by managed to whisk the baby out of the pram a second before it shattered.

I often stayed with Granny. But, she lived in a rather spooky house which was large and rambling.

Her eldest son Edward was an extremely courageous boy, who ran away from Eton and lied about his age in order to join the Army. He was very badly wounded but was determined to go back and fight for his country. He was killed at the Battle of the Somme.

All over the house were glass cabinets, with his baby clothes, bootees, sailor suits, school uniform and his Army uniform, which was rather disquieting for a young child.

I have always had a phobia of very large paintings and tapestries, and it persists to this day. One whole wall was covered with a tapestry of a larger-than-life Alexander the Great landing in one of the lands he conquered. It left me so terrified I was quite unable to eat – even though there were always my favourite sandwiches of asparagus rolled up in brown bread and butter.

I was equally terrified at my Uncle Porchy's home, Highclere Castle, where in the dining room there was a massive

MY PATERNAL GRANDMOTHER BETTY BEAUCHAMP
WITH HER ELDER SON EDWARD, WHO WAS KILLED
IN THE FIRST WORLD WAR.

portrait of King Charles on a white charger, which I could hardly bring myself to look at. Even now, I look at it with some disquiet.

I don't know whether these sorts of phobias can be inherited but my sons both went to school in Dorset and, on one of their days out, we took them to Wilton House, where there is a room full of very large Van Dykes. After just a couple of minutes in the room, my eldest son Simon, who must have been about 15 years old at the time, turned white and said: "I must get out of here". After we left, I asked him why he had needed to go out and he replied that he had found the portraits terrifying and felt that they were coming down on top of him, which is strange, because I had never mentioned my fear to either of the boys. I wonder whether it is a phobia with a name – or is it too rare?

I also used to lunch regularly with my maternal grandmother in London, who gave me my favourite meal of fried fish, which I always referred to as 'brown fish', and a bowl of home-made vanilla ice cream. That until one day my mother asked me what I had eaten for lunch and I innocently replied: "Brown fish, ice cream and crème de menthe." She did not approve. I believe that was the last time I lunched there without supervision. At that time, I was six years old. I was very fond of her. She was the daughter of Baron Alfred de Rothschild and Mrs Wombwell. She was small and very beautiful, with perfect features, and was known as 'the little Dresden shepherdess'. She married the 5th Earl of

Carnarvon, who lived at Highclere Castle. He was the famous archaeologist who, with his partner Howard Carter, discovered Tutankhamun's tomb in 1922.

His sister, Lady Burghclere, lived in the Dower House at Highclere. It was the most beautiful house beside a very large lake surrounded by wonderful azaleas, which were reflected in the water. Lady Burghclere was always known as Auntie Quack Quack because she was forever feeding the ducks on the lake, where we caught some fairly large pike.

My Grandfather had two half-brothers who were both very clever. Mervyn became a successful ambassador and Aubrey was a mid-European expert.

I saw quite a lot of my grandmother. Highclere Castle had been turned into a hospital for wounded soldiers during the First World War. She loved her work and seemed to have an instinctive gift for healing, although she had had no training. After the war, she opened a nursing home called Alfred House, opposite the BBC in Portland Place, London. Her nursing home became quite famous – Princess Marina, the Duchess of Kent, had her children there and the Gloucesters always used it, as did the Queen of Spain.

It was an excellent nursing home and had a first class reputation among all of the top consultants. Most of the nurses were very pretty. A lot of them came from Ireland and they wore pale crushed strawberry uniforms with a starched white veil.

There was a famous surgeon, Lord Moynihan, who

only operated in Leeds, where he lived, or at Alfred House. One day, a nurse went into the theatre. She came out and commented to the sister: "I didn't know Lord Moynihan was operating today".

"What do you mean", came the reply. "He died this morning." But the nurse had clearly seen him there, packing away his surgical instruments.

Almina was very involved with her work. A friend took her to the opening night of a play on the Life of Pasteur and of his successful discovery of a vacine for rabies. At the moment in the play when he is about to give his 1st injection on a human with rabies there was total silence in the theatre until a piercing shriek from the font row "The damned fool, he hasn't sterilised the syringe!"

Almina called her nursing home Alfred House after her father Baron Alfred de Rothschild. Baron Alfred adored his daughter. He lived in a very large London house in Seymour Place. In those days Curzon Street was a cul-de-sac and the area which now leads straight through to Park Lane was where his house was situated. He had the most superb collection of paintings, known as the Little Wallace Collection. It included three studies by Gainsborough, a Peter de Hooch and many other works of art. The furniture was exquisite and the china priceless. When he died, he left his whole estate to Almina. I believe it is the only time that a Rothschild fortune has been left outside the family.

She was extremely extravagant. It cost a great deal

to run Highclere Castle in the manner that she liked, and financing both her hospital and Alfred House, took up a large part of her funds. She also had an extremely expensive hobby. She would buy beautiful old houses, with a view to living in them, do them up throughout in lavish style and then decide she was bored, sell them off and buy more. These days, it could be turned into quite a profitable pastime but, in those days, it was a disaster. Every time she required more finance, she sold one of the items from Seymour Place until, at the end of her life, they had all gone. However, I think it is fair to say that she never gambled. Her money was mostly spent on healing people and making their periods of illness happier and more comfortable.

She was also very fond of parties and entertaining. On one occasion, she was at a ball given by Sir Edward Cassell for his granddaughter Edwina, who eventually became Lady Mountbatten. Granny so enjoyed it that, in the middle of the dancing, she said to my mother, "Let's give a ball of our own tomorrow night." Mummy was horrified and asked how they could possibly manage it, at which point Granny said: "Well, I've already invited everyone here, so I'm sure we'll have a wonderful time."

The party was to be held on a Friday night at Seymour Place. Grandfather always left on the six o' clock train from Paddington every Friday evening to go to Highclere. But on this particular Friday, he must have known that something was in the air. He was an intensely private person, who only enjoyed parties if they were given for the Egyptian King and his other Egyptian friends. Instead of going out at his usual time, he hovered, so that each time my grandmother asked the butler whether his Lordship had left the house, the answer came, "No, not yet."

Eventually, the butler came up and said: "His Lordship has left but, as he was doing so, he passed ten dozen lobsters on the back stairs!" The next day, when my mother joined him at Highclere, he simply said with a smile, "I do hope you're not too tired."

After my grandfather's death, my grandmother married a most charming man, Colonel Ian Dennistoun. I loved him. He was great fun and I used to enjoy going to stay at the house they had in Brighton. He was mostly confined to a wheelchair as he had broken his hip very badly slipping on a highly polished floor and it never properly healed. His hobby was sailing model yachts and we spent hours together racing these very intricate crafts up and down the lagoon in Hove. He died relatively young in Granny's nursing home. I was aged about ten at the time and was absolutely heartbroken.

My paternal grandfather was in the Navy. He once wrote a letter home from the China Sea saying that it was so boring there, the men's only source of entertainment was knocking the weevils out of the biscuits and racing them. He ultimately became chairman of Lloyds, not once, but twice – a very unusual feat.

Around the time that he left, Lloyds were diversifying

My Mother
Evelyn Herbert

by Orpen

to include many other areas of insurance as well as marine. He told all the members of the family never to become a name at Lloyds because he fervently believed that the diversification would lead to difficulties and possibly the death of the institution. Many years later, he was proved right. My grandmother came from Columbus, Ohio. Sadly, both my grandfathers died before I was born.

MY FATHER BROGRAVE BEAUCHAMP MP. 1930s

I was very fond of my father, although I didn't see him very often as he was chairman of a number of big companies, as well as an MP and parliamentary private secretary to the under-secretary for Foreign Affairs, Dick Law, the younger son of Bonar Law who had been Prime Minister from 1922 until he died in 1923.

Among my father's Companies was one called Pyrotenax. The French had invented a non-flammable cable, but they had been unable to manufacture it in long enough lengths. My father and some of his friends bought the patent for England and set up a factory in Newcastle. After some experimentation, they managed to find a way to produce it in long coils.

The product was sold all over the country, including to Coventry Cathedral. Years later, when it was bombed, the electric light system never stopped working!

I adored my mother, Evelyn, who was called Eve. She had a wonderful sense of humour and was highly intelligent and great fun. We had some wonderful times together. When I was young, she was very strict as I was an only child and she didn't want me to become spoilt. My parents were away a lot, so I also had a Nanny.

My parents gave me a little black kitten called Sooty, which I was devoted to. One holiday, while we were away, she had kittens in my dolls' pram. When we got back, I noticed I had a new pram but I don't think the exact reason why was ever explained to me.

A few years later, they gave me a Norwich Terrier puppy called Tom Thumb. This eight-week-old puppy came down from Norfolk in a basket and my father met the package off the train at Liverpool Street station. Tom Thumb arrived a shaking little bundle of brown fur and remained my constant much-loved companion for 15 years.

I spent my time playing with friends in the park and exercising Tom Thumb. I learned to play tennis, rode and swam a great deal. I took my bronze lifesaving medal with a friend. The examiner said 'fall in', so we did – with a very large splash!

TOM THUMB
ARRIVING FROM NORFOLK AS A CHRISTMAS PRESENT

I learned to ride at Miss Smith's school, which, at the time, was the place where the young went, hoping to become equestrian geniuses.

I went to a school with all my friends, run by Miss Faunce and Miss Lambert, which taught the most civilised of subjects – literature, history, history of art and poetry. I am still immensely grateful for the poetry I learned there. To this day, if I'm stressed or bored, I am able to recite those poems to myself and it still gives me a lot of pleasure. The more weighty subjects, such as mathematics, tended to be bypassed by the school, which suited me just fine.

I had no brothers or sisters but my cousin Penelope Herbert, my Uncle Porchy Carnarvon's daughter, was exactly the same age as me. Every weekend, along with our nannies, we would catch a train from Paddington to her home at Highclere Castle where we always had the most wonderful time. We would ride over the downs and have picnics and we had our own electric car, called the Redbug, which was imported from

My Cousins
Penelope and Porchy

Le Touquet. It consisted of floorboards, two pedals, a steering wheel and two remarkably uncomfortable seats. We soon discovered that if you turned the steering wheel quite sharply to the right, whoever was riding in the left hand seat, would be catapulted out – most satisfactory, especially when giving a ride to someone we didn't much like! We also used to raid the greenhouses for peaches and nectarines until one day we got locked in and had to wait to be rescued by the head gardener, whose wrath was so terrible; we never tried it again.

On the outbreak of war, my entire London school was evacuated to the home of Lord Shaftesbury at Wimborne St Giles. Life in Dorset was quite idyllic – a few desultory lessons in the morning, then a game of tennis, netball or rounders in the afternoon, while weekends were spent picnicking in the wonderful Dorset countryside.

During the war, my Mother worked very hard – first at the WRVS, as the chief buyer for the Lord Mayor's Fund, which distributed clothes, blankets and other necessities to bombed out families. It was an enormous task and, at that time, it was not at all easy to find the quantities of goods required. However, Marks and Spencer were magnificent, and introduced her to all of their suppliers. Sometimes, in order to deal with a supplier, she would have to creeping up rickety old stairs into attics with bombs falling all around.

She then moved on to the Red Cross and worked in their department based at St James's Palace, where she interviewed the relatives of prisoners of war, and helped to send out letters and parcels. When the prisoners were repatriated, she met up with a number of them and, sadly, caught tuberculosis. The doctors failed to recognise it. For two years she kept saying, "I'm so tired, I can't drag myself about," until, eventually, she had only half a lung left. She had to spend a year in bed on terrible antibiotics, which she said made her feel as though she was permanently in a rowing boat on a rough sea. She did pull through, mainly through sheer willpower, and managed to get some of her old life back.

In the holidays, I had to stay at Highclere Castle by myself because, by that time, Penelope had been sent to live with her American relations in Virginia. My uncle was away in the Army, as was my cousin Porchy. My father was MP for East Walthamstow and he felt it was only right that he and my mother should stay behind and endure the same discomforts and bombing as their constituents.

The Castle was a frightening place and, in order to preserve the generator, I had to creep up to bed by torchlight. The night watchman came around two or three times a night. He had a clubfoot, which used to go boom–bang, boom–bang, much to the annoyance of my dog Tom Thumb.

I kept waking up in the middle of the night, convinced that someone was sitting on my feet, although I didn't think it could be anything too sinister, as it didn't seem to have any effect on my dog. Some years later an American relative was staying at the Castle in the same room. I asked him had he enjoyed his stay and he replied that he had, but had been unable to sleep, as someone kept sitting on his feet.

I believe it may possibly have been a Herbert family member, who was injured in the Crimea and spent many months being nursed in the room until his death. To this day, if you go into that room, you may find an impression on the eiderdown, as though someone has just had a nap.

When I left school, my mother thought it advisable for me to learn shorthand and typing. In retrospect I am sure that cooking and bridge lessons would have proved far more useful! My parents had bought a house at Virginia Water and every morning I bicycled up a virtual mountain to get to Queen's Secretarial College at Englefield Green. I was always late. But of course, when I was in no hurry at all, I flew downhill all the way home.

Nearly all my friends were at the same College, so there were lots of opportunities to have a marvellous time. A number of them had cousins or brothers at Sandhurst. We used to meet up at the weekends and chat, dance to the gramophone or save a whole month's worth of sugar coupons to purchase a tin of golden syrup, then sit around the fire munching our way through a pile of drop scones.

It was at that time that I was lucky enough to be invited to a dance at Windsor Castle. Several of my friends at the college were also invited and we were collected in a minibus and driven to the Castle. On arrival, all the young guests were assembled in the hall and Sir Piers Leigh, the Master of the Household, climbed on a chair and addressed us all, explaining the finer details of etiquette – how we should behave and how we should address Royalty. This was immensely helpful, as we were all quite young and inexperienced. My partner Alan Breitmeyer was a marvellous dancer and we were having a lovely time waltzing. Halfway through the evening supper was served and we were a bit desultory going in. When we got to the dining room, it appeared as though all the tables were already occupied. We headed towards one with two spare seats before realising with horror that it was the Queen and King George's table. The Queen turned around and very sweetly invited us to join them. Though we sat down with some trepidation, the Queen had a wonderful gift for putting people at their ease and we were soon very much enjoying ourselves again.

It was a wonderful party – we danced until 4am then, as the sun rose over the Thames, we heard the music of a piper as he strode up and down the walkway beneath the windows. On the way back, in the bus, we were all in very good form and my friend, Sarah Beckwith-Smith, started dancing in the aisle and clowning about. We were all convulsed with laughter until the driver stopped the bus and informed us that he couldn't possibly continue with so much noise and we had better all be quiet.

When wartime came, I had an ambition to join the Wrens – I think mostly on account of the uniform. I was just 17 when I was called up. It meant going to Mill Hill for two weeks' inauguration into the ways of the Navy, a process that also involved a few domestic chores. The chores didn't go too well. The first morning I was handed a bucket of water and a solid white brick and told to use them to wash the back doorstep. I had no idea whether one melted the brick in the water, or rubbed it directly onto the scrubbing brush but I took a chance and tried the latter, which resulted in my being hauled over the coals for producing a very streaky step. Next, I was asked to iron the officers' white shirts and given an iron and a very small ironing board with which to perform the task. The first shirt seemed quite satisfactory until I came to fold it up. There wasn't a lot of room to manoeuvre, so I put the iron down on the floor, oblivious to the fact that floors in nissan huts are made of asphalt – a fact that only became apparent to me when the iron started to sink slowly. It took four of us to lift it and it came out with an almighty plop, covering everything with tar. The iron itself was a complete write-off.

I'd had a sheltered upbringing and suddenly to be sleeping 72 to a room in double decker bunks was quite an eye-opener. To my amazement, a lot of the girls slept with gin bottles under their pillows. There was one particular girl we all thought was likely to come to a sticky end and, indeed she did, becoming one of the victims of the notorious murderer Neville Heath, who disposed of his victims in a bath of acid.

At the end of the two weeks at Mill Hill, each of us had to decide in which category we wanted to work. Having just passed my driving test, I had a picture of myself at the wheel of a car, driving some dashing Admiral around London but, unfortunately, all of the glamorous jobs had already been taken and there were only two vacancies left. One was kitchen work. Having joined hundreds of people in breakfasts of greasy fried bread and eggs swimming in fat, I didn't think the kitchens were for me. The other option was P5. That was it. No one was even allowed to know what it was until they got there.

Due to absence of hard facts, weird rumours abounded. One was that the Wrens in P5 had to work eight hours a day in water up to their necks; another that they were to be dropped behind enemy lines – a prospect I did not particularly relish. I signed up!

Still not knowing what P5 was, I put my signature to some very frightening Official Secrets Act documents, stating that, as long as I lived, on pain of imprisonment, I would never tell anyone what we did – not even my parents. The way I saw it, it was that or the fried eggs, so the decision made itself.

Two friends, Susan Dugdale and Penelope Palmer and I signed up at the same time, collected our uniforms and climbed onto a bus into the unknown. We drove some considerable distance out into the country before arriving at a large red brick house, standing in its own grounds and completely surrounded by a steel fence, with a single heavily guarded entrance.

We had arrived at Bletchley Park, the centre of the UK decoding operation.

The Germans were using a very sophisticated machine to communicate with all their different operators, the Enigma machine. All messages sent by the Germans were intercepted and run through our machines but, unless our machines were set to exactly the same settings as the sender's, all that came out was a jumble of random letters.

Some very brilliant boffins had managed to decode some of the German messages, helped in no small part by human nature. If you go to buy a fountain pen, your instinctive reaction when trying it out is to write your own name or initials over and over again. The German operators were no different. One came to know, for example, that the operator in Cologne always set his machine at his wife's initials. From that, it was possible to decipher his whole message.

I worked at a computer that was 12 feet long and eight or ten feet high, which had huge banks of drums, whirring away. Whenever the drums stopped, you wrote down the letters, sent them through to the operators' room and hoped they were the correct answer! However, there was one incident that came very close to destroying all our efforts. We took a message that said that the Scharnhost was leaving Norwegian waters, so a battleship was sent to intercept, carrying the Admiral in charge of the area, who wanted to be in at the kill and so went aboard for the afternoon. Unfortunately, the ship was not of a class that would usually carry an Admiral, so the Germans immediately knew that the Navy had advance notice that the ship was being moved and they responded by changing their codes. It set the work at Bletchley back many weeks, as the Enigma machine was enlarged to have extra drums, so that the number of combinations of letters available became, not 52x52x52 but 52x52x52x52.

THE ENIGMA MACHINE
BLETCHLEY

By the end of the war, I believe we were deciphering every single communication sent by the Germans within an hour and Churchill said that our work probably reduced the length of the war by two to three years.

At the time, no personnel in uniform were allowed to travel by public transport. When we were given a long weekend off, I would have to get from Bletchley Park to Virginia Water. This involved hitch hiking via Aylesbury and Windsor. All the drivers were wonderful but I have the feeling that it is not a means of travel you could use quite so successfully today.

Bletchley, was near Newport Pagnell. We thought we were there for good and were well established, getting about by means of our own bicycles and a pony and trap. We even had a canoe.

When we returned from work one night, we were told that within the next 48 hours we would all be moved to a depôt at Eastcote near London. This was a real emergency. What do you do with a pony and trap and a canoe in 24 hours? In the end, the bikes were loaded onto a train and, somehow, a local farmer was persuaded to take the pony and trap. I'm not sure what became of the canoe.

Unfortunately, I had caught jaundice before joining up and, due to the irregular hours, the illness returned and I was invalided out of the Wrens.

Once I had recovered, I went to work for the Red Cross in London, where I had the most charming boss, Mrs Young, who was great fun to work for. She once told me a story about her grandson. His guinea pig had died and he dug a hole in the garden to perform a burial ceremony. She heard him say in the most solemn voice: "In the name of the Father, and the Son and into the hole he goes!"

I was working there when the war ended and it was the most marvellous time, with a great bubbling atmosphere of peace. For me, life became one long round of parties, dances and theatres.

Princess Elizabeth and her sister Princess Margaret, together with Prince Philip, came to stay at Highclere for a weekend shooting party. Because my cousin Penelope was ill, I was designated hostess. I was very nervous in advance but they were so nice and appreciative and it turned out to be great fun.

Unfortunately, when Saturday dawned, it was pouring with rain, so the shooting was cancelled and we had to play indoor games instead. We played a lot of Racing Demon. The Princesses were brilliant at it and so quick it was impossible to win against them.

We also played 'The Game', which is a form of charades. I am a hopeless actress, so I found this agony and consequently kept letting the side down.

In the evening, the Princesses played the piano and sang. They were so good that, had circumstances been different, they would easily have made a name for themselves in the world of entertainment!

My mother came from a racing family and loved racing. Her father had started a highly successful stud farm at Highclere, which he left to her brother. It had always been my uncle's ambition to breed and own a Derby winner. He bred a beautiful colt, which they named Blenheim. But my grandfather died young, at the age of 56, and there were crippling death duties to be paid. A lot of possessions had to be sold - including Blenheim – who was bought by the Aga Khan.

The horse duly won the Derby and, although he lived to 93, Carnarvon never did manage to own a Derby winner.

He married a very pretty American called Catherine. She was sweet and kind – and both her children and I adored her. But until she married, she had never had any contact with racecourses or with any form of gambling. The exciting atmosphere of the track rather went to her head and she ultimately became a very large punter.

One day, they had all gone together to Chester Races and, immediately after the last race, went to the cloakroom to collect their belongings before catching the train to London. Catherine turned to my mother and said, "I didn't tell you before because I knew you would be so angry, but I had £2,000 on that last winner, and it has got me out for the week." Carnarvon was a man who shook all over if he had so much as a fiver on a horse. As they walked out of the cloakroom, he was standing outside rubbing his hands with glee and saying, "The objection to the winner sustained. That makes me £20 up."

Little did he know that his wife had just lost £4,000. My mother said that she and Catherine laughed all the way home in the train from pure hysteria. Uncle asked what the joke was and my mother had to tell him that she didn't think

AUNT CATHERINE   UNCLE PORCHY CARNARVON

HIGHCLERE CASTLE

he would appreciate it.

As I grew up, I used sometimes to go racing with her, especially to Royal Ascot. But my only real piece of luck was on the Friday of one Ascot, when my parents couldn't go, so I was sent down by train. Although my mother had a very small appetite, she always felt it was important to have something to eat if one was going to be out all day. She ordered me some sandwiches from a very good fish restaurant called Wiltons in King St, St James's, which was run by a great character called Marks.

We were quite friendly with Marks and, as he wrapped up my sandwiches, he said to me: "Tell your Mum 'Lucky Jordan for the Wokingham'." Later that day I discovered that Lucky Jordan was in fact a 66/1 shot and placed my maximum bet – £1 – on the nose. Lucky Jordan duly obliged – the only problem was that I had forgotten to tell my mother. I didn't say a word but, when next she went into Wiltons, Marks asked her how she had enjoyed Lucky Jordan. "Lucky Jordan?" she said, mystified. "Yes, I sent a message with your daughter." Suffice it to say, I was not flavour of the month!

Lord Carnarvon was also a very good amateur rider and won a number of races. He was popular with the racing public, who nicknamed him 'Lordy', and in close finishes, you could always hear the shouts of "Come on Lordy! Come on Lordy!"

My mother only owned one racehorse, which had been bred at the stud and was given to her by her brother. It was a little mare called Miraculous and, to her great delight, went on to win many races.

One day we were racing and Prince Ali Khan, whose racing colours were brown and green, had a much-fancied runner. He had a very large bet on it, only for it to come in last. One friend asked another: "How is Ali taking it?" The reply came back: "He turned a delicate shade of chocolate and green!"

We had a friend, Baron James de Rothschild, who liked to plan his own breeding programme for his racehorses, which, on the whole, were not very successful. At one meeting he had a horse called Snow Leopard, which he really fancied, and unfortunately, it did not run well. A friend of his met him in the paddock afterwards and said: "What are you going to do with Snow Leopard?" He said: "I'm going to change its name to Slow Leopard."

Years later, my son Edward looked in on me and said: "I think Richard Shaw's horse, Hello Dandy, is going to win the Grand National. Richard was a person with whom we had both played a lot of golf, along with his wife, Yvonne. Edward said he thought it would be fun to have a tricast on the race – a bet predicting the first three runners home. I told him he must be nuts – it was nearly impossible to get the winner of the National, let alone all the placed horses. He said: "It will only cost us a fiver," and I replied, "Well, you might as well cut your fiver up and put it in the waste paper basket." But he insisted that it was just a bit of fun and, anyway, he had already picked out the horses.

In the event, Hello Dandy won quite easily and the other two horses Edward had picked out finished second and third. For our fiver, we pocketed £17,500. That was about the only piece of success that he and I had together on the horses.

I married Michael Leatham, but it was somewhat delayed. When I was just 15, my parents had given a dinner party to which he was invited. He had worked for my father's firm before he joined the Army and his parents were great friends of my parents.

I was at school near Salisbury while Michael was stationed on Salisbury Plain, so he rang the headmistress to ask her permission to take me out.

"Certainly not," was her reply and, even though he pleaded that he was a friend of my father's, she said, "I don't care who you are. None of my girls go out with young men."

It ultimately set the romance back seven years, because it was that long before we met up again. We met at a point-to-point where Michael came over and said, "I don't expect you remember me." But, of course I did. We went out to dinner that night and never looked back.

After Michael and I got engaged, my maternal Grandmother very kindly invited Michael and me to lunch at The Ritz. As she looked around the dining room, she would constantly notice people she knew and remark, "Look, there's old so-and-so." Then she would not say, "we used to dance together," or some such comment but, "I took out his gall

MICHAEL ON OUR ENGAGEMENT

bladder in 1935 – it was a most interesting operation," or "she had a terrible appendectomy, you know."

Michael was the sort of person who would faint if a hypodermic appeared on the TV. He became greener and greener until I had to ask Granny please to change the subject.

Michael's father, Chicot Leatham, had commanded the Grenadier Guards in the First World War and George V sent for him and said that he wanted a new regiment to be formed titled The Welsh Guards, so Chicot formed the new Regiment and commanded it. Consequently, all Leathams have served in the Welsh Guards ever since.

Michael's mother Menda Ralli was Greek and was the daughter of the famous banking family. His Greek grandmother used to come to stay and was in the habit of pretending to be so deaf that she couldn't hear anything that was said to her. That was, until there was some juicy piece of gossip that she really fancied, when she could miraculously make out every word!

Menda was originally married to Lord Arthur Hay, who was killed in the First World War. His brother Edward was killed in the Second World War in the Guards Chapel. He was reading the lesson when the building was hit by a Doodlebug. Strangely enough the whole Chapel was destroyed, except for the altar and the amazing mosaic behind it.

Menda and Arthur had one daughter, called Jean, who later married William Makins, Roger Makins' cousin. Chico and Menda had one son called Michael who was followed by his sister Elizabeth. She married Anthony Hanbury and they

MICHAEL'S FATHER, COLONEL 'CHICOT' LEATHAM,
IN FULL DRESS UNIFORM OF THE
WELSH GUARDS

by Orpen

had two girls and one boy, who were approximately the same age as Simon and Edward, so all the children used to have great fun together.

When Michael left Eton in 1936, he went to work for my father in his construction business and always swore that he started his working life in the sewers beneath the East End of London.

When the war came, he joined the Welsh Guards and became a Major, serving throughout the war despite being shot through the chest by a sniper's bullet that missed his heart by half an inch.

Years later, an American friend had some relations over to stay and asked us to dinner. One of them was a terrible bore and spent the whole meal boasting about what he had done during the war. At the end of his monologue, he turned to an exasperated Michael and said, in the most patronising tones: "Tell me, Mr Leatham, what did you do in the war?" Having given distinguished service with the Welsh Guards and not caring to be patronised, he said, without a smile: "I put the holes in the doughnuts." The American replied: "That's mighty interesting."

We were married in St Margaret's, Westminster. Sorry to say, I remember very little about our wedding, save for my uncle, who was a punctilious man, sitting on the end of a pew, watch in hand, as I arrived at the altar five minutes late.

My parents gave us a superb wedding reception at The Ritz – we were the first people ever to have a reception there.

Our Wedding
St Margaret's, Westminster
28TH November 1949

33

My father, Brograve Beauchamp, with
my mother-in-law, Menda Leatham,
at our Wedding

My mother, Evelyn Beauchamp,
at our Wedding

My father's political associates, my mother's friends from the racing world, my friends, Michael's regimental colleagues and all of his mother's friends and relations were there – a very large number of people.

We left the party late and spent the night at The Savoy. At the time, they were building the Festival Hall on the South Bank so we spent our entire first night of marriage serenaded by the sound of the pile drivers at work.

The next day we went to Paris, where we spent the week doing a few museums and a lot of restaurants.

From there we went to Lisbon, where one of my father's political friends was the British Ambassador, and had very kindly said he'd keep an eye on us.

He entertained us lavishly and, one day, took us for a picnic. At one point, Michael leapt out of his seat, turned to the ambassador and said: "Paul, your son has just stuck his penknife into me!" Totally seriously, the Ambassador replied, quite calmly, "I hope it wasn't the small blade. I keep that for fruit," which was hardly diplomatic for a member of the diplomatic corps! Michael felt he'd really got his own back, when on a trip to a restaurant in a lovely old port near Lisbon, the wretched boy took a straw and sucked up a great gulp of crème de menthe – only to blow it all over his mother's fur coat.

While we were there, we met up with Tim Consett, a regimental friend of Michael's to go to the local casino. We had a wonderful night and we all went home quite happy. But we heard the next day that he had gone to bed only to decide that it really was his lucky night, got up again, dressed and returned to the casino. By the time he re-emerged, he couldn't even afford to tip the commissionaire and had to borrow the money for his taxi home.

We returned from Lisbon on the maiden voyage of a small liner, which at the time we thought would be rather fun. It turned out to be anything but. Somehow the air conditioning system had been connected to the funnels, resulting in the whole ship smelling of acrid smoke. To make matters worse, there was a funny smell in our bathroom. Michael found a hole in the floor and poured water down it, thinking it might help, but all that happened was the people in the cabin below were soaked to the skin.

The whole journey lasted only three days but I was not a good sailor. Michael had been told that champagne was good for seasickness, so I took great care to drink quantities of it every day. It was only when we docked that we learned, it was not the champagne that was beneficial so much as the bubbles, and I could equally well have lived on soda water.

We returned to live in Michael's flat in Seymour Place near Marble Arch.

While I had been on honeymoon, my mother and father had been in New York on business. When my mother came back, I declared with great confidence, "Now I'm married, I'm a marvellous cook. You must come to lunch." She was surprised but said, "that would be lovely."

When the day came, I decided I would serve fried fish, a dish I had been practising. I prepared everything beautifully, she arrived and we started gossiping. Suddenly there was the most frightful smell, which turned out to be the result of my leaving the fat on the hot cooker.

We had to have the fire brigade out and move out of the flat for a week. All our clothes had to be cleaned and, somehow, the smell even managed to find its way into sealed tins.

Our next home was a house in Victoria Road, Kensington. I remember one day asking my uncle, whose life revolved around the Ritz, to lunch with us. He arrived a quarter of an hour late, which was most unusual for him, saying by way of explanation that he was terribly sorry but I hadn't told him I lived in the country!

My husband Michael was a wonderful man – very loving, kind and patient, with a great sense of humour. He had the ability to say the funniest things with a completely straight face, having a roomful of people or a whole dining table convulsed with laughter. Although he was very strict with them, he adored his sons.

It was while we were living at Victoria Road that Simon was born. He weighed nine and a half pounds. I had wanted to have him at home but my gynaecologist Sir William Gilliatt insisted that he would never allow first babies to be born at home because of the possibility of complications. It turned out to be very lucky indeed.

I went to Sir William because it was he who brought me into the world. I have a scar on my back and he asked me how I had come by it. When I told him he had cut me during the course of my mother's caesarean, I think he wished he hadn't asked!

Gilliatt's Hospital was King's College and, as he was also the Queen's gynaecologist, the Americans had sent the hospital an isolet for the birth of Prince Charles, as there was very little specialist equipment in British hospitals to treat delicate babies.

Simon was very ill at birth, as he had breathed before he was born. He was immediately put into the isolet and I couldn't see him for ten days but it was thanks to the isolet that he survived. It is interesting to note that, if a baby is deprived of oxygen for a few seconds in this way, as Simon was, he'll tend to have a slight tremor of the hands later in life. However, had he been starved of oxygen for a longer period, he would likely have had cerebral palsy.

When we were allowed to leave hospital and return to Kensington, I had a marvellous old Irish nanny of about 70. She was such a snob that she used to go out early and run with the pram all the way to Hyde Park Corner, in order to turn around and be seen coming from the direction of Mayfair!

Simon was christened in the Guards' Chapel. Michael's step- sister was to be godmother but we had not realised that she had just developed an illness that made her shake. Throughout the ceremony, the poor baby was rattling as though he was sitting on a pneumatic drill!

There was another nanny whom I had known in the past as she looked after a friend of mine, Anne Richmond, and she came to me wondering if we could give her employment. She was quite prepared to do the cleaning and hoovering and I thought, what a splendid idea to have two nannies. It turned out to be not such a good idea because the pair never stopped fighting, day and night, until in the end we had to let her go.

Although the dining room at Victoria Road was tiny, you could just squeeze eight people in, so we did a lot of entertaining and had masses of friends to dinner, including Martyn and Pinkie Beckett. Martyn was a superb pianist, who could sit down and play any tune you requested, straight off the top of his head. He became Simon's godfather.

We also often hosted Nigel Fisher and his wife, Gloria. He was an MP and, when we had our second son, Edward, he agreed to be his godfather. A lot of Michael's Welsh Guard friends often used to pop in, as well as my old school friends.

It was around this time that Michael took me on holiday to Italy, where we visited many museums, art galleries and churches and got stiff necks from looking up at all the marvellous paintings on the ceilings!

We went to a lot of restaurants, but I'm not sure we got the best out of them, as we both had difficulty translating the menus.

One day, as we were going through the Uffizi, a crowd of people were coming from the other direction and we saw that one of them was Princess Elizabeth, surrounded by a large number of dignitaries. She saw us standing against the wall and came over to have a chat, much to the surprise of all the dignitaries.

Prince Philip had recently been sent to sea and, upon our return, we felt that Princess Elizabeth must be feeling very sad and lonely, so we decided to invite her to dinner, along with five of her best friends. She accepted graciously and we all squeezed into the dining room. We had a very good cook, who produced a delicious dinner of lobster neuberg followed by lamb accompanied by tiny peas and carrots, picked that very morning in my father's market garden. It is amazing the difference in taste between freshly picked vegetables and those that one buys in the shops.

After dinner, it was decided to go on to our favourite nightclub, the 400 in Leicester Square. As the Princess had not brought a lady-in-waiting with her, I went in the royal car and Michael had to drive as fast as he possibly could to Leicester Square in order to be there to greet us when we arrived. It was no mean feat, as the royal chauffeur was no slouch when it came to driving at pace. We had a lovely time and I hope we managed to give Princess Elizabeth a happy evening.

Some time after Simon was born we decided it would be nicer all round to live in the country. We sold the Kensington house to some people who, I understand, are still living there and moved temporarily to a flat just around the corner. One day we were all having lunch. We didn't hear a sound, but during the course of the meal, a burglar had walked in and stolen my fur coat. We never discovered who took it and nor did I manage to get it back.

We thought it would be ideal to farm somewhere adjacent to London, so that Michael could still commute. For months we searched for a suitable farm but in every case, either the house was good and the farm was terrible or vice versa. One particular farm I went to see had a lovely house but its owner had clearly not been near the farm for many weeks. He threw open the door of one barn and proudly announced, "This is where we fatten the pigs" but all we could see there were mounds of little dead piglets.

We eventually found a nice dairy farm in Kent, with a beautiful Queen Anne House. We made an acceptable offer and arranged for a survey. The survey was a disaster. It concluded that the arrangement of the chimneys was such that it was amazing the house had not burned down. We withdrew our offer and gave the vendor a copy of the survey explaining our reasons. I don't think he can have read it because I heard nine months later that the house had indeed caught fire.

In desperation, we bought a Queen Anne house on a friend's estate north of London, although only just 25 minutes from Marble Arch, it was right in the middle of the countryside and from the upstairs windows the only glimpse of civilisation was the dome of St Paul's.

The location of Old Park Farm had just one snag. It only had a quarter of an acre and what do you farm on a plot that size? We wanted to build a garage with a flat over for a gardener and applied for permission, stating that we were going to be a market garden. Planning turned us down. We were in the midst of the Lee Valley and even our tiny acreage was considered an unwanted rival to the established growers.

After rejecting chickens and turkeys, we decided on pigs – not that we knew a thing about them. We erected a rather smart pig house, using impossible-to-follow DIY instructions. After three weeks of struggling, Porky Palace was complete. But where were we to find the first inhabitant?

We were told of a dispersal sale 20 miles away in Essex and borrowed a friend's lorry for the day. Armed with the information that the first lots always fetched the least, we set off early. We had just slowed down behind a pony and cart carrying a load of manure, when, suddenly, a series of deafening bangs came from the engine. The poor pony bolted and was last seen distributing manure liberally over Essex. The lorry, meanwhile, stopped and refused to start again. We sent an urgent SOS to the AA, who eventually arrived. A cable had become dislodged. It took all of five minutes to rectify the problem but by the time we arrived, the sale was nearly over and there was only time to buy a rather attractive large black and white sow in pig, who was due to farrow in two or three weeks.

We got her installed in Porky Palace and the baby piglets came along two weeks later. We kept running out to see if we could help but she just looked as us with disdain as if to say, "I've done this before. Please go away and leave me alone." It is fascinating watching piglets being born. Within 30 seconds of birth they are all lined up at the milk bar.

With that experience under our belts, we thought we'd expand and built four more Porky Palaces and some fattening pens to fatten the babies up for bacon. When fattening pigs, it's essential to weigh them every week and make sure they are putting on the necessary 10lbs per week. But this is easier said than done, as a piglet's one idea in life is to escape. We literally ran miles trying to contain those wretched little pigs!

I was in hospital when Edward was born, Michael arrived to see me, not with a bunch of flowers, but with the pigs' weighing book tucked under his arm. He felt it would give me far more pleasure than flowers and, of course, he was right. Old Park Farm had become Old Pork Farm and this pig business had really got under our skin.

When we had first arrived at Old Park Farm, we had considerable difficulty in finding any staff to help in the house, having no shops nearby and being tucked away in the country, miles from a main road. We eventually managed to find a Spanish couple, who spoke not a word of English. They were with us when our little dog was due to have puppies. The puppies arrived over a weekend, while we were away. Upon our return, the Spanish man greeted us on the doorstep with great excitement, saying: "The little peoples are come!"

We bought a linguaphone record of Spanish but had barely got as far as the Spanish for scrambled eggs, when they decided to leave.

I applied to the job centre and was put in touch with a most charming English woman called Evelyn, who was really wonderful – a very hard worker, an excellent cook and devoted to our two boys. There was just one fly in the ointment, which I didn't know about at the time.

Evelyn turned out to be a lunatic in the truest sense of the word – she was affected quite dramatically by the full moon. Being unaware of this, one day fairly early in our relationship, I walked into the kitchen and just in the nick of time, saw a saucepan flying towards my head, which she had thrown. Luckily, being used to games, I was able to catch it. We had to take great care not to give any dinner parties or make any social arrangements during the phase of the full moon but, once we had grasped this vital lesson, Evelyn became one of the family, and we were all particularly fond of her. Her lunacy was a small price to pay for her excellence in every other way.

SIMON
AGED FIVE

45

Both boys went to the local pre-prep in Enfield and, as they grew up, they took an interest in the pigs. Sometimes we took them to the livestock shows, which they thought was marvellous.

As I had enjoyed my school life in the beautiful countryside of Dorset, we then decided to send Simon to Sandroyd prep school in Tollard Royal. Eventually his brother Edward followed him to the same school. There is an altar rail in the Chapel at Sandroyd on which is carved the date Simon started there with his initials SAML and, on the other side of it, the initials EAML and the date that Edward left the school.

We had great fun taking the boys out of school at weekends. Arming ourselves with eggs and sausages and a Calor gas stove for cooking, we used to go for winter picnics. It was an excellent school and both of the boys were very happy there. Edward was always very good at games and at his pre-prep he was Victor Ludorum. When he joined Simon at Sandroyd, he grew into a very good cricketer, and made the first 11, and he enjoyed playing rugger as well.

It was customary at Sandroyd for the fathers of the first 11 to play a match against their sons once a year. Unfortunately, at Eton, Michael had never held a cricket bat, as he had spent all his time rowing on the river. He went down to school in his Viking (wet bob) tie and was greeted by the Captain of the Fathers' side, saying: "I can see you're not going to be much good."

When his own boy went in to bat, each father had to

bowl and, even though Michael hadn't bowled since his prep school, he was determined to do Edward proud, so he took a long run before discharging the ball, which fell at his feet, much to Edward's chagrin. He thought he'd try something different, so he took another long run and threw the ball at the wicket but it missed, sailed over Edward's head and shattered the windscreen of one of the cars in the car park. Poor Edward didn't know where to look!

We bought a larger pig farm near Luton, to which I commuted two or three times a week. It provided accommodation for 200 bacon pigs as well as a large number of sows. Eventually it dawned on us that it would be more exciting to show pigs and then sell them for breeding stock. So we held a dispersal sale of all our non-pedigree pigs and started a herd of Landrace pigs. Landrace had only recently been imported to this country from Sweden and were very much the new fashion.

We had any number of traumas – most of them due to bad pigmen. We did have one splendid man who, whatever you said to him, would reply: "I thought so meself." What we didn't know was that, when he sat at the shows with a glass of beer in his hand, it was in fact constantly being topped up with shorts and we only found out on the way home one day when he managed to overturn the lorry in a ditch. After that we employed a new pigman.

We bought ourselves the champion boar at a show. He was very expensive but, as he left the lorry, he slipped and broke his back, so he never produced a single litter of piglets and finished up as overpriced bacon.

The next crisis occurred when a number of pigs that were kept out of doors started to die. Desperately worried, we were recommended to contact someone who had what was called a black box. We sent samples of blood and hair and waited anxiously for a report to come back as to the cause of the illness. In due course the message made its way back that we were to take the pigs out of one particular field, as there was a buttercup growing there that was poisonous to them. We followed that instruction and, sure enough, we had no more trouble.

We eventually found ourselves a first class pigman and the herd went from strength to strength, winning championships all over the country, including the Royal, Smithfield, the Dairy Show and the Toronto Winter Royal.

I sometimes used to show some of the pigs myself, and the head pigman and I had a running battle. He felt that if we had something special, it should go in last, whereas I felt it should go in first. One day, we were at a show together. The class we were showing in was starting and the pigman was nowhere to be seen. I thought to myself, "my moment has come", and I opened the door of the sty to bring out our biggest and best sow. She dashed out between my legs, taking me with her, and proceeded to race round the ring, with me clinging on by her tail. I could hear people all around shouting, "Come on Lester". She finally collapsed with exhaustion and

I was able to step off, feeling more than a little foolish. The pigman didn't speak to me for a week!

It was important to be at all the shows so we used to start on the road in May and finish in December after Smithfield. Showing was really very exciting. Boars only have one thought in their minds – to kill another boar – yet all that we were allowed to control our animals with was a plywood board measuring approximately two feet by 18 inches. It was quite a difficult task not to either be bitten or be speared by their long tusks.

Before being shown, our pigs used to be bathed, polished, brushed and shined to a brilliant white and, for that reason, our pigman's nickname on the circuit was Mr Omo. Our herd prefix was Thundergrove, so Michael became known in the show ring as Mr Thundergrove.

We won the championship at the Royal Counties Windsor with our boar. Her Majesty was walking down the livestock lanes and we waited in the pens for her arrival. I was standing in the pen, trying to control our boar, which was only separated from the large white boar next door by a very flimsy fence. They spent the whole time trying to get at each other. Just before the Queen reached us, our boar whipped his head around and caught my leg. Luckily, the Queen didn't see that I was dripping blood the whole time I was talking to her. She stopped at our pen, admired our boar and spoke to the head pigman Mr Breakspear. He even shook her by the hand – it was the proudest moment of his life and something he never forgot.

When the pigs had reached the correct weight for pork or bacon, we had to transport them to the factory. On one occasion, we were taking a load of pigs to market. Driving through Waltham Cross, we suddenly heard a lot of hooting behind us. The doors of the van had flown open and, unbeknown to us, there was not a single pig left inside. We drove back down the High Street and found several of them queuing at a bus stop. The strangest thing about it was that no one seemed to have noticed.

We exported quite a lot of livestock to Japan, Canada, Romania and Russia and even received a Christmas card from the Kremlin. One batch was loaded to go by air to Romania. The pilot taxied down the runway and then he taxied back. He said to the pigman, "I didn't mind them smoking in a non-smoker but, when they sat on my lap, I had to draw the line". It turned out they had burst out of their crates and were all charging up and down the aisle.

Romania is a very interesting country from a farming point of view. While the population, on the whole, lived in fairly basic dwellings, the pigs were housed in virtual palaces with electric lights and underfloor heating.

It is interesting to note that countries have various different requirements. The Russians only buy stock from litters of ten or twelve. The Japanese are only interested in having sows with evenly arranged teats, which is strange because the little piglets really like them more randomly dispersed. It is quite a sight to see the Japanese crawling on the floor underneath the pigs' tums, counting and measuring their teats!

When the Russian buyers came to the farm, they were always followed by two minders. Even while on a buying expedition, they were obliged to report back to the Russian Embassy every 48 hours. As a result, if they were buying, for example, Aberdeen Angus in Scotland, even if they hadn't finished, they would have to come all the way to London to report in and then go all the way back.

It was important never to judge a client by appearances. One day, we had a client turn up in a very old knocked about Ford. He said he wished to buy two or three gilts and a boar.. We showed him round the commercial stock, but at the end, he asked, hadn't we got anything better? We took him to our show stock and he bought four gilts, plus a boar.

After that, he then asked, had we got any fields nearby in which he could land his helicopter? He usually travelled by helicopter, but it was in for servicing, so he had been forced to borrow his foreman's car!

Since our pig operation had grown so considerably, it seemed stupid and inefficient to live so far away, so we purchased a very nice house with 120 acres at Finchampstead in Berkshire. It was about eight miles from Broadmoor and, unfortunately, on the day we moved, one of the inmates had escaped and there were police as far as the eye could see, causing our Nanny to remark that she didn't think it was a very nice neighbourhood.

Before we could move the pigs down, we had to build Porky Village, which had lots of different accommodation for our various needs. It had all mod cons – underfloor heating, infra red lamps and facilities for the pigs to spend a penny because pigs, when they are allowed, are actually very clean animals and would never think of soiling their beds.

We also built our own ring in which to show the pigs off to prospective buyers and to accommodate our own annual sales.

At feeding time, pigs make a tremendous noise shouting for their food. In a bacon shed of 200 pigs, the noise is deafening. Some farmers don't feed their pigs on a Sunday, partly because they think the rest will do them good, but also to save on labour. The interesting thing is that, at the time when they should be fed, they all start up in unison. Only when the food does not arrive for five minutes do they shrug their shoulders and go back to sleep.

It was a lovely farm. We also had sheep and it was fascinating to watch the sheepdog working. We grew potatoes and had a splendid machine that went up and down the rows, while people stood up on a platform sorting a constant stream of potatoes into good and bad before putting them in sacks. One terrible year it rained and rained and it was impossible to get the machine onto the fields. We were desperate to know what the forecast was, so we rang the weather station at Bracknell and said: "When will it stop raining?" The reply came back: "Is it raining?" I asked if they had looked out of the window recently and was told: "We don't have any windows here."

In the end, we had to bring in the Army to pick our potato harvest. They were absolutely marvellous – twice as quick as the machine and laughing and joking non-stop. We were forever grateful to them.

Simon progressed to Eton, which he very much enjoyed, making a number of good friends. Like his father before him, he never took to cricket, so he too became an oarsman or 'wet bob'. It was lovely to go to the open day on the fourth of June and see everyone in their best clothes with huge picnics lining the riverbank to see the boats come down. The boys would be rowing, then, at a certain place, they would have to stand up and, without upsetting the boats, all hold their oars aloft. This was a fairly tricky operation and often ended up with some of the oarsmen getting very wet! The procession of boats was always followed by a magnificent display of fireworks.

Our boys had a wonderful time on the farm. There was a large field at the side on the house on which they charged about in go-karts and, eventually, as they grew older, they used to go to the car auction and buy old bangers for a fiver for the same purpose. Funnily enough, it was not such a good idea because, when the time came to take their driving tests, they already thought they knew it all and consequently both failed two or three times.

Edward also had a pony, which he used to ride at

gymkhanas and which I always thought he enjoyed. That was until one day he fell off in the field and I said to him: "Get straight back on, otherwise you'll never ride again." "Oh good," he said. And that was the end of that.

Adjacent to the Finchampstead property was the cricket ground and one year it was to be the scene of the village fete. As we lived alongside, we felt we should make some contribution. Michael was invited to open the fete and we took the decision to donate a baby pig as the prize for the bowling. The winner could then either take the animal or the equivalent of its value in money. We took the pig to the bowling alley, where it clapped its trotters and decided to try to dig its way to Australia, which meant we were less than popular.

While we were in Finchampstead, we learned that the local shop in the Wokingham Road was up for sale. On the principle of 'try anything once', we decided to buy it.

It was a very small shop and included the village Post Office. People were having to queue and could never find what they wanted on the shelves. Turnover was extremely poor and after two months struggling, we decided to expand and built a small supermarket attached to the original premises, bringing in the professionals to design it.

MICHAEL WITH SOOTY

Supermarket talk seemed a language all its own but we quickly learned that it amounted to this: The things people have to buy, like soap powder and sugar, should go on the bottom shelves. Things that are non-essential but are nice to have should be placed at eye level to induce a spot of impulse buying. It was very interesting.

All the same people shopped there one week and the

following Monday, we opened self-service. During that first help yourself week, the turnover quadrupled. It was all great fun but very hard work to keep the shelves full at all times and the shop immaculate. We had an extremely good manager – something that is absolutely essential, because it is a very tricky trade. For instance, we found that the bakeries supplied the big supermarkets daily on a sale or return basis and provisions not sold would be taken back and redelivered to the smaller independent shops on the second day. We only discovered this practice by chance, when one supermarket neglected to take its price tags off a batch of buns.

We also found it a very dishonest trade. If you ordered sides of bacon, for example, at the same time as four sides were coming in the front door, one could quite easily be walking out of the back if you didn't watch out. The ice cream deliverer would always visit small shops that closed for lunch at around one o'clock. As a result, if the staff were not on their toes, they would return at 2 to find a vanilla lake on the doorstep and the poor old proprietor would have to place a whole new order.

It is very important to do everything possible to try to stop people taking things off the shelves and slipping them straight into their shopping bags. However, you have to be careful not to stop people until they have actually left the shop, as they can always accuse you of unfairly embarrassing them when, "of course", they were intending to pay all along. There was one otherwise very sweet old man who, we noticed, would help himself to half a bottle of whisky every single week. When we asked him why, he explained that his wife had cancer and the only thing that seemed to take away the pain was a tot of whisky, but he did not have the money to buy it for her. We let him have the bottle that was already in his possession but told him that we would be most grateful if he would mind doing his shopping elsewhere in future.

One week the manager was ill, so I had to get behind the delicatessen counter. I had spent the morning cutting up chops and slicing ham when a customer came in and said she would like some of the tongue. I slapped it on the slicer and switched it on. The machine seemed to be slicing away but there was no tongue coming off. Suddenly I realised that I had put it on far too fast and the tongue was flying off the end of the slicer and straight into the lady's shopping bag! I said nothing but slowed it down and wrapped the proper amount up as subtly as I could. I wonder if that could have been the origin of buy one get one free!

We sold the shop on after a couple of years and, although at times it had been a traumatic experience, and very hard work, we really missed it. The boys always used to come and help fill the shelves but they also used to help empty them, filling their bags with supplies whenever they were going back to school!

When Simon left Eton, he did not go on to University, but had a gap year, spending his time waterskiing. He was an expert waterskiier and joined a waterskiing circus, giving performances all around the country before heading off to Australia.

As he had only just turned 17, Michael and I didn't want him going out there without having something arranged, so a friend of ours got him a job in an iron ore mine north of Perth. It was 110 degrees in the shade and there were 2,000 men and one woman working there. He had been told that he would be using iron ore handling equipment and, having taken a course in tractor and crane driving, was really looking forward to being in charge of some serious heavy machinery. But his first letter home said: "The only trouble is that the ore handling equipment is a shovel." He shovelled all day long, covered in red dust, as the iron ore passed by on a conveyor belt.

He then went on to work on the big Japanese tugs, bringing cargo into port. After six months, having received extremely high wages in the mine, he was able to buy a car and set off to drive around Australia.

At one point on his travels, we hadn't heard from him for some time and we were getting worried, so we spoke to our friend in Australia to enquire whether he had heard how Simon was getting on. He said he hadn't heard, but he would try and find out. Soon after, Simon went into a bank to be told by one of the clerks that he was wanted by the police. In fear and trembling, he went along to the nearest police station. The sergeant looked up from his writing and said sternly:"You haven't phoned your mother."

He had a great time in Australia and I felt it turned him

from a boy into a man. The down side was that, after enjoying all that freedom, it was very hard for him to knuckle down to work in an office in the City. I take my hat off to the way he managed to do it.

At the time, we also had a house and a farm on Jersey and kept a herd of Jersey cows. Jersey is a beautiful island and the people there are charming. We really meant to sell the farm in England and go and live in Jersey but, unfortunately, Michael caught rheumatic fever and was advised that he should never live by the sea, so we just used to go over in the holidays.

It has the most wonderful sandy beaches, but some very dangerous currents. We went to St Brelades Bay and, before we had time to unpack our picnic, one of the swimmers had got into difficulties. The coastguard went out on a rope attached to a big wheel to pull him in but it transpired that both the swimmer and the coastguard were drowned.

Jersey also has the most lovely cows, which are much smaller than the English variety because, owing to the lack of land, they are not exercised over large areas but are tethered and only eat the grass around them. It is amazing how they have kept their quality over so many years, because the breeding programme seems to have been quite haphazard. It wasn't so much a planned programme as a case of; the cow is ready, it's a full moon, we might as well go to the bull next door.

We had 20 milking cows and one of our cows produced approximately the same as a Friesian, which was very unusual. As Jersey has iron subsoil, it is inclined to have thunderstorms.

One day the cows were in the cowshed when lightning struck. It bounced down the milking lines and threw all of the cows onto their backs. I'm glad to say they were not badly damaged but the milk production dipped considerably for a week afterwards.

When we first started going there, the flying was quite unpleasant because, in those days, the planes were not pressurised and sometime had to climb quite high. Once we decided to catch a plane from Southampton, which was quite convenient. The boys took one look at the planes on the runway and said they weren't going anywhere in those matchbox toys. It was only as the years went by that the runway was extended and larger planes were able to get in.

We eventually decided to sell the pig herd and we held a dispersal sale. People came from all over and our champion boar fetched a world record price and appeared on the ITN News that night.

I had a major car accident in 1974. It was St Andrew's Day and I was motoring along on my way to fetch my son Simon from Eton. I was travelling on the main road from Bracknell to Ascot and there were a few shops on the left with a small lay-by in front for cars to pull in. As I approached, a man pulled out from the side. I thought he was going straight on but, as I went to pass him, he performed a U-turn in middle of the road and, although I swerved, I ran out of road and we collided. The impact must have been very severe, as his car ended up a good 40 or 50 feet away from mine. At first, I thought I had been blinded because, as I looked out of the windscreen, all I could see was what I took to be a creamy grey mist. In fact, what had happened was that the bonnet had popped up and was pressed so firmly against the windscreen that all I could see was the paintwork. I think I must have been knocked out for a short time because I hit my head very hard on the windscreen.

It was before the universal use of seatbelts and, to make matters worse, I was driving a Triumph Herald, in which the driver's seat folded forward to let the back passengers out.

I asked the other driver, "Didn't you hear my horn?" and he replied that he was very sorry but he had forgotten to put his hearing aid in.

By the time I went home, Michael had heard the news and returned from his shoot near Winchester and a taxi had gone to fetch Simon.

We sat down to lunch and I ate an enormous meal of roast chicken. It turned out to be the last proper meal I would have for a month. I later discovered I had severe shock, a fractured skull and a damaged back. I also developed pneumonia and it took me a very long time indeed to get back to normal.

Following my accident I was kept in bed for some time. When I was feeling better, Michael took me for a holiday to the south of France, an area we had always loved. We had a marvellous time visiting restaurants, playing golf and generally whiling our time away.

There was one particular restaurant we loved at St Paul de Vence, where one could sit out on the terrace, overlooking mile upon mile of vineyards. Another marvellous restaurant, where the food was superb, was called the Bon Auberge. For some reason, the car was temporarily out of action and we decided to visit the Restaurant, which was, I suppose, six or seven miles away and we hired a Vespa for the purpose. I had never been on a motorbike in my life and I was literally shaking with fear. We were in a queue of traffic going past a shop, when I happened to look in the window and catch a glimpse of the pair of us. I said to Michael: "How funny we look," whereupon we both laughed so much we nearly fell off. That was the first and last time I have ever been on a Vespa.

We didn't go to the Bon Auberge too often, as the food was very rich and very expensive. One day we were there when an American lit up a cigar in the middle of his meal – between the first and second course – much to the horror of the French, who asked would he kindly extinguish it.

While we were in France, we saw a little house by the golf course at Mougins that we both fell in love with and Michael bought it for me, feeling that more frequent holidays would probably do me good. We kept it for a number of years, invited our friends there and played a lot of golf at the local course. But one of the things I most enjoyed was visiting casinos.

There is nothing so exciting as walking into a casino absolutely sure that it is your lucky night. Actually, in all my life, I have only had one really lucky night. I used to play baccarat, which consists of eight players, sitting either side of a table, with a banker in the middle. The banker deals cards to the punters and then to himself. He turns them over after the players have placed bets on who will have the best cards.

On this occasion my luck started to run and, whenever someone is lucky at a table, the rest of the players usually start to follow them. I had an amazing 21 coups against the banker. In those days, the maximum sum allowed at that casino was £3,000, per person, per coup, so that, by the time it ended, 16 people were all betting their various maximums and the cost to the casino was enormous. In fact, the baccarat had to close down for four days afterwards.

Of course, for me it was a disaster, because I kept thinking how easy it was to win. I couldn't have been more wrong.

Another time, we decided it would be fun to go for a holiday in Morocco. The journey involved changing to a smaller plane in Casablanca, where it was absolutely pouring with rain. It was a terrible little plane, with no steward, just a small cupboard from which, if you wanted a drink, you had to help yourself. It was so bad I made poor Michael agree to return by train, even though it was an eight-hour trip in a coal truck with wooden seats.

I found the food in Morocco quite good but very difficult to eat, as you had to sit on the floor and eat with your fingers. Funnily enough, the fingers can stand far less heat than the mouth, so by the time the pigeon pie was cool enough to handle, it was too cold to eat.

On the whole, we were not very lucky with trains. We went by train to the south of France because of my dislike of flying. I said that it didn't seem sensible for us to sit in the train while it travelled all around Paris, so why didn't we get out and do some shopping and rejoin the train later? What we failed to take into consideration was the fact that it was the rush hour. We couldn't get onto a bus to get back to the train station and we couldn't find a taxi. We eventually rushed onto the platform just as our train was disappearing into the distance. For some reason, I started running after it, at which Michael called after me: "There's no point running – you'll never catch it!" Once again, we ended up sitting on a goods train that stopped at every station between Paris and Cannes.

Another time, we decided to go with a party of six friends to Le Touquet for a long weekend of gambling and golf and we chartered a plane to leave from Croydon. We weighed in as normal and then we waited, and waited, and waited. After an hour, becoming rather exasperated, we asked the reason for the delay and were told that, having weighed the passengers, they had had to send for a smaller pilot!

After that, Michael, the boys and I used to go to Le Touquet on the excellent service from Kent, which allowed you to take your car on the plane.

I was always one for getting to the head of every queue, much to the annoyance of Michael and the boys, who liked to saunter at their own pace. When the flight was called, I would race ahead across the tarmac to make sure we got four seats together. On one occasion I did just that, then, after a while, there was a bit of a commotion on the plane as some other people seemed unable to find their seats. I was asked whether I had a ticket and it was only then that it was explained to me that I was on the wrong plane. That particular plane was flying to Birmingham. I was forced to get off and walk all the way back across the tarmac, much to the pleasure of the boys, who enjoyed the spectacle immensely.

One day Michael went out to lunch with a very old friend of ours who said he was just off to book himself, his wife and his children on a cruise around the Mediterranean and why didn't we come too? Michael agreed and returned home looking rather sheepish, as he knew how I hated boats. Trying to make light of it, he said in a jolly voice, "We're all going on a cruise next year!" I replied: "No we are not," but he said, yes, we definitely were – because he had already booked it and, anyway, it would be nice for the boys.

For six months I grumbled every day and was most objectionable about it whenever the opportunity arose but, I must admit, I enjoyed every moment of it. The cruise took us all around the Greek Islands, Albania and Turkey. I was particularly interested to visit Albania because my great uncle Aubrey Herbert had once been invited to be King of the country. He said he would only do it if the British government agreed to support him while the country was getting on its feet.

They refused, so he turned the offer down. He was a great expert on mid-European countries and spoke five languages. While fighting the Turks during the Great War, one Christmas Eve, he walked across no man's land waving a white flag. He proceeded to speak to his Turkish counterparts and explain that it was Christmas, so would they kindly stop shelling for two or three days, which indeed they did. He then calmly walked back to his own trenches.

Ours was also the first tourist boat to be allowed to visit Russia. The crowds turned out on the quayside waving their newspapers in the air in a very friendly way but we saw that there were officials going around knocking the papers out of their hands.

We also visited Yalta and Odessa. The only snag was the food on the boat, which was truly disgusting. Even Michael lived on nothing but cornflakes.

The cruise finished in Venice and we were staying there for a few days when both of the boys developed the most appalling sore throats. We called for the doctor, who examined them and said: "I don't know where you've been but I haven't seen anything like this since Belsen." Both boys had scurvy, the ailment that sailors used to get for lack of vitamin C. It was a shame because I had arranged for Simon and me to go to lunch with a very pretty girl, the daughter of a Maharaja, and her mother. Simon had tea with her while he was at Eton and took rather a shine to her. I had thought there might be a very nice dowry but the scurvy put paid to that!

We went to one Greek island, Mycene, and the guide told us we were at the spot from where the Rallis left to make their fortune, which was fascinating to us, as Michael's mother was a Ralli. I loved Greece but it was so unbearably hot that we could hardly appreciate the wonderful buildings like the Acropolis because, from the moment we stepped off the plane, the air burned our lungs and we vowed to return some other time. We also loved Turkey, which, in a way, was less overcivilised. Travelling out into the country we felt people were still living as they had lived for centuries.

At the beginning of our married life, Michael played golf at weekends and so I generally didn't see a lot of him. I eventually came to the decision that the only thing was to learn to play golf myself, although up until then I had only played tennis. I really caught the bug and soon I was practising every day, until I was even keener than Michael had ever been. When we went to Berkshire, I joined Sunningdale and the East Berks and the Berkshire. I dread to think how many miles I must have walked around those courses. Sunningdale is an absolutely wonderful course – very difficult, and not one you could ever tire of playing. At that time, it was also a course famous for its gambling. A lot of members used to play for money and enjoyed taking on the club's famous pro, Arthur Lees, for large sums. He would always give them a lot of shots, leaving them sure that they could win. But, of course, on the whole, they didn't, as he was so very good. There was one famous occasion when Lees and his opponents were coming up the 18th all square, both standing to win or lose £1,000 depending on the result. They reached the green and there was some mud in the way of Lees's putt. He swept it aside, but some remained, and diverted his putt away from the hole, losing him the match. He stormed into the secretary's office and demanded to know what that mud was doing on the green. The secretary looked up and said: "That wasn't mud, Mr Lees, it was Mr X. He was scattered there this morning." Now members may be scattered on the fairways but never on the greens.

I worked very hard at my golf, to the detriment of more important things, and eventually by pure luck managed to become Berkshire champion. It only happened because two of my friends, who were both infinitely better players than myself, were ill at the time of the competition.

Another time, I was playing in a competition when my friend and playing partner asked me if I had taken out insurance against a hole in one, as it could work out to be quite expensive by the time one had bought all the other players a drink. I laughed and said: "Good Lord, no. I'm never going to be likely to get a hole in one!" "Well, you never know," said my friend. "Stranger things have happened." Believe it or not, only two weeks later at East Berks, I did get a very expensive hole in one.

The only place that Michael and I ever argued was on the golf course. His drives were never very straight and frequently used to curl into the woods. I would go in after them, give a great slash and fail to move the ball. He would say that he told me not to press and I would reply that I wasn't accustomed to playing the ball from such places.

Unfortunately, the long and short of it was that he gave up the game and I carried on, so we still didn't get to see all that much of each other!

I played a large number of matches. To my mind, there is nothing so exciting as a really close match that goes right up to the 18th. A friend of ours, Tim Holland, who used to sit in the front window of the golf club's lounge, would watch people coming up the 18th. Whenever I came up, he would get his friends to lay bets on whether I had won or lost, as my face was always absolutely inscrutable! This was down to my mother's training. She always said it was most important not to gloat when one was winning or to look sulky or depressed in defeat. "Meet with triumph and disaster and treat those two impostors just the same," as Rudyard Kipling said.

One of the lovely things about Sunningdale was that we were allowed to take our dogs with us. Sometimes, there were more dogs on the course than people. There was a hut half way round where you could get anything to drink from coffee and soup to champagne and from sandwiches to sausages to eat..

The dogs were all known by their name, plus that of their owners, so mine was Brandy Leatham. Their likes and dislikes were all noted and their favourite meals were ready by the time their owners reached the hut. It was very civilised.

I was forced to give up golf for a time due to an extremely bad back and when it was slightly improved, I continued playing with the aid of a steel belt, which was both uncomfortable and restrictive.

One day we went to dinner with some friends, Nigel and Elizabeth Bingham. Nigel's eyesight had become extremely bad due to glaucoma and he said that he had been advised to visit a healer called Len, whose practise was in south London. Eventually, he had been persuaded to try it and was absolutely delighted by the results. His eyesight had improved and the glaucoma had even receded up to a point. Nigel suggested that I should go to Len for my back. I was very sceptical but he insisted that it wouldn't matter whether I believed in Len or not, because his healing worked just as well in animals as in humans. He told me not to go unless I was accompanied, as the treatment tended to make its subjects sleepy and I would need someone to drive me home.

So it was that, eventually, Michael and I set off to see Len. The very first thing he said to me was: "Take off that steel belt.""I can't," I said, "My back will snap out again and, anyway, it's extremely painful without it." But Len was adamant. "No," he said. "You can take it off now and you won't need it any more." He then stood for approximately 20 minutes with the palm of his hand hovering about an inch or two away from my back. I felt a feeling of deep heat and the occasional tremor, as though from a small drill. At the end of 20 minutes, he said: "That's fixed. You can play golf as much as you like but I'd like to see you again in two or three weeks to give you one more treatment."

True spirit healers, as they are called, never charge for

70

their services because they feel their healing is a gift from God and, if they exploit it commercially, it may disappear but, of course, they have to live and so grateful patients always leave a discretionary donation.

Len was quite right and, from that moment on, I was able to play golf with no further problems and, without the restriction of the belt, my swing improved immediately.

Some time later, Michael was experiencing a very bad pain in his back and the doctor diagnosed a stone in the kidney. An x-ray revealed a very large stone, which the doctor said would have to be operated on. As a last resort, we went back to see Len who said that it was indeed a stone but, not to worry, he would carry out a psychic operation.

As Michael was getting into bed that evening, he screamed in pain and said it was as though a red-hot knife had entered his back. But from that moment on, he had no further troubles and, when he was next x-rayed, the stone had mysteriously disappeared.

Len has since died, but he trained a young woman called Dorothy to follow in his footsteps and she has proved to be just as accomplished a healer.

When our son Simon slipped a disc right in the middle of taking his accountancy exams and just three weeks before his wedding, the doctor told him that he would require six weeks bed rest to recover so, in desperation, we sent for Dorothy. She stayed with him for about half an hour and, when she left, he seemed as right as rain. We were still nervous, though, and as he had to get back to London for his exams on Monday, we sent him back in an ambulance, something he described as a terrifying experience. They motored along with sirens blaring and blue lights flashing and Simon asked them why the hurry, as he was certainly not in need of emergency treatment and the driver explained that the crew wanted to get back in time to see the rugger! The next day Simon was fine and, after a week, he was back water-skiing.

Dorothy has become a great friend and whenever there is an emergency, hers is the first name that comes to mind. She believes that everybody has the gift of healing to a greater or lesser extent but someone like myself may only be sufficiently powerful to be able to help animals. In that sense, she said, healing is rather like water divining. Anyone can be a dowser but most people don't realise it because they have never tried it. In light of Dorothy's comments, we decided to arm ourselves with a hazel twig and set off marching around the countryside. It was fascinating to see the twig leap when adjacent to water and leap in the other direction when adjacent to metal. We became so hooked on our experiment and its success that we travelled absolutely everywhere with our twig in the hope of making further exciting discoveries.

We went to stay at one rather smart house where our luggage was unpacked and our clothes laid out for us. There, on the bed, adjacent to Michael's dinner jacket and black tie was our hazel twig. We never did discover what the butler supposed it was for! Nevertheless, it really is an exciting phenomenon and one that's well worth experimenting with. Unfortunately, following another serious motor accident, I had to give up golf for good and I deserted the green grass for the green baize and took to bridge. But more of that later.

One of Michael's favourite hobbies was shooting. He used to get quite a lot of shooting at Highclere, which is one of the best shoots in the country. One day they were there duck shooting and there was a most annoying guest who used to hold everyone else up at the pheasant shoots by demanding that people search for his pheasants, when everyone knew perfectly well that he hadn't hit a thing.

We were all waiting round the lake and someone shouted, "What's the hold-up?" Another guest replied, as quick as lightning, "We're looking for a mallard imaginaire," which was rather clever.

We had some marvellous Labradors, who would go for miles through the deepest woods to bring back a wounded pheasant. One Labrador habitually ate everything – particularly golf balls. After a number of operations to remove them, the decision was taken to coat the golf balls with bitter aloes to deter her but she just licked her lips and said; "I like these golf balls even more with bitter aloes sauce!" One day, she even ate a bath plug with the chain still on it and got herself all plugged up.

One day when we were out shooting in Essex, there was a cabinet minister among the party. A message came through that Harold Macmillan wanted to speak to him urgently and would he take a car back to the house. When he returned to the shoot, he knew everyone would be agog to know what it was all about. He had a very good sense of humour and said it was only a message from the Congo, "When are you sending more troops, the last lot were delicious!"

MICHAEL SHOOTING IN ESSEX

One of the most interesting things we did in the 1970s was attend the British Museum when Her Majesty the Queen opened the Tutankhamun exhibition. My grandfather had discovered the tomb with his Egyptologist Howard Carter. It is generally supposed that Carnarvon was merely the sponsor of the expedition but this is entirely incorrect. He was, in fact, a well-versed archaeologist and had already carried out one season of excavation prior to meeting up with Carter.

It is interesting to note the background to the discovery of King Tutankhamun's tomb in the Valley of the Kings in November 1922. In Egypt, the King's name is pronounced Tutankarmoun, denoting that he was beloved of the god Amunra. He was the son of Akhennaten, who was married to the famous beauty Nephatiti, who never bore him a son – his mother was in fact one of Pharaoh's lesser wives named Kiya.

After Akhennaten's death in the 17th year of his reign, a Pharaoh of whom very little is known, ruled for three years. It could even have been Nephatiti herself. Tutankhamun came to the throne at the age of nine and was immediately married to Nephatiti's youngest daughter, probably to unite opposing factions within the royal house and maintain Nephatiti's own power.

Had the motor car not been invented, the wonderful treasures from the tomb would probably never have been seen. My grandfather was a very clever man, with many hobbies including photography, archaeology, history, racing and anything mechanical. He was fascinated by the invention of the motor car and imported the second one into England. The car travelled so slowly that a man waving a red flag walked ahead to warn the public of the danger.

Years later, I was told by a shop assistant in Piccadilly that she had lived in Highclere village as a child and remembered how everyone would line the streets to see the terrifying monster go by. Mothers would tell their children: "If you are naughty, Lord Carnarvon will come and take you away in his motor car," which, apparently, was an appalling threat!

Some years later, he had a Bugatti and, while driving through Germany for a rally, he came over the brow of a hill and found an ox cart right across the road. He had a bad smash and was very badly injured. The car landed on top of him and he was face down in the thick mud. His chauffeur, who was thrown out of the car by the impact, managed, with the help of people working in a nearby field, to prise his face out of the mud, only to find that he had stopped breathing. He threw a bucket of cold water over him and he came to. The chauffeur then continued to hold his head up out of the mud until further help arrived. Incidentally, he remained as chauffeur to the family until the day he died many years later.

Carnarvon's accident and subsequent ill health caused his doctors to tell him that he could no longer winter in the cold English climate. He decided to go each winter to Florida until it occurred to him that he would be bored in Florida with nothing to do, so he changed his mind and instead chose to winter in Egypt. Being a very erudite man and a keen amateur archaeologist who was always seeking new knowledge and was unable to relax, he studied Egyptology.

At the time, Egypt was full of Americans and Europeans, all excavating and searching for hidden treasure. Carnarvon obtained a licence from the Director of Antiquities in Cairo and, with a team of workers, he set out to try his hand. After one season, he had found nothing but a mummified cat in a cat-shaped sarcophagus so the next season he returned to the

Director requesting a licence for a better area. The director suggested that Carnarvon should meet up with an English friend of his, Howard Carter. Carter's family lived in Norfolk and his father was a talented artist, who made a living painting dogs, horses and various other pets for the local gentry. He was too poor to send his son to school but educated him himself and had taught him drawing and painting.

One of his neighbours, Lady Amhurst of Hackney, heard of young Carter's skill at drawing. Her husband had brought back a number of antiquities, which he wanted listed and illustrated. He was so impressed by Carter's talents that he recommended him to the Egyptian Museum, where he was put in charge of twenty empty tombs in the Valley of the Kings. All went well until, one day, a party of very drunk Frenchmen started desecrating one of the tombs. Carter was sent to deal with the problem. He was, by nature, an aggressive man, totally lacking in tact and diplomacy. The French, who have wielded great influence in the Cairo Museum since Napoleonic times, demanded that Carter apologise. He refused, saying he had only been doing his duty and consequently he was sacked and took up painting full time. He made a small living taking the tourists around the tombs and selling some of his paintings.

Approximately 20 tombs had already been discovered but all had been robbed and stripped of any significant treasures, probably at the time of burial.

Carter and Carnarvon hit it off immediately. Carter had been looking for a financial patron and he, in turn, was able to offer Carnarvon the professional status required by the Antiquities Department in order to grant him access to a better area for excavation. Carter had done considerable research over the years and was certain that there were further tombs still to be found in the Valley of the Kings. Together they applied for a licence, only to find that the concession they required had already been issued to an American called Theodore Davis.

It was not until 12 years later that Carter and Carnarvon began to excavate in the Valley of the Kings. It proved a colossal job, moving away all the top rubble of the Valley until bedrock was reached. The digging season ran roughly from October to April, due to the excessive summer heat.

The area of the concession was two-and-a-half acres. There were, of course, no machines and all the rubble had to be carted away by boys with baskets on their heads, who never walked but ran because they received a token for each basket of rubble they tipped away and exchanged their tokens for money each evening. Carter, who could look down into the Valley from his house, wrote that it looked like an ant heap with very disorganised ants running hither and thither. The whole site was divided into grids and each grid had to be completely cleared before they could move on.

I think my main impression, many years later when I visited the Valley of the Kings, was sheer amazement and admiration that anybody could have undertaken such an enormous task. There had been a few clues found in the area – some jars and pots bearing the King's name had been unearthed – but they had probably been discarded by contemporary robbers who had been disturbed. In 1912, Davis had uncovered a pit with some funeral equipment and some papyrus, which he had sent to the Metropolitan Museum in New York. It was not until 1921 that these were finally studied by the museum and Carnarvon received a very excited letter. It was the ancient Egyptians' custom that the priest and embalmers should have a feast in the tomb before it was finally closed. Translated, the papyrus said that the tomb of King Tutankhamun was now complete and that eight people partook of the feast, eating five ducks, two plover and a leg of mutton, all washed down with beer and wine. So there were definite indications that the tomb was adjacent.

The priests had tried unsuccessfully to protect the mummies by constantly moving them but still the robbers persisted. The same family of thieves had for generation after generation robbed the tombs from 1000 BC until 1875 AD, when they fell out amongst themselves and one reported the location where they had hidden the mummies. Officials found more than 50 mummies stacked in a cave.

Five seasons of digging went by with no positive clue as to the location of the young King's tomb. At Christmas 1921 Carnarvon sent for Carter and, sitting in the library of Highclere Castle, broke the news that he could no longer afford to finance another season. Things in England had become more difficult, he had many staff to pay at home and could not afford to keep paying out the £5,000 per year that the dig was costing. Carter pleaded for one more season, saying that there was only one small triangle left to excavate and even pledging that, if necessary, he Carter, would finance the last year himself. Carnarvon eventually gave in but with the proviso that this was to be definitely the final effort. He felt depressed that so much time, money and effort had so far proved useless. Obviously they had been wrong and there was nothing there – it had all been a waste. The following October he told Carter to clean up the final corner and pay off the hundreds of workers. He and my mother were returning home.

At the time that a tomb was being prepared, workman's huts were built adjacent to the site. As a last desperate effort, Carter decided to demolish the foundations of the huts built following the death of Rameses, who lived later than King Tutankhamun. When he returned to the site the next day, there was complete silence in the valley. Carter was worried that there had been an accident because the boys would normally be chatting and laughing. Then the foreman ran up saying: "Master, master. I think we have found some steps under the huts." Carter went to see. There were indeed steps leading down to a door with the young king's seal still intact. Carter ordered that the steps be filled in and a guard put in place until such time as his patron could arrive. He then rushed straight home to send a telegram to Carnarvon.

As he approached his house, his servant came running

out carrying a small bundle of yellow feathers. Carter had previously bought a canary to keep him company and all the boys had said that the beautiful golden bird would bring them luck and take them to the tomb. The servant explained that he had heard squeaking and fluttering and had arrived just in time to see a cobra eating the canary. The cobra is the serpent always seen worn on the forehead of the kings to protect them through life. The servant was visibly shaking and said: "Master, you must not enter the tomb. It is dangerous – this is a sign of the wrath of the gods." But Carter just told him not to be such a fool and to just make sure the cobra was no longer in the house.

While having tea at Highclere with my mother, Carnarvon received the telegram. It read 'Think have discovered entrance to magnificent tomb with seal intact. Awaiting your arrival.' Very loyally, Carter had covered over the steps until Carnarvon returned. One can only imagine his impatience, his worries, his doubts and hopes as he waited. Travel in those days was very slow – by P&O steamer to Alexandria, then by train to Luxor. From Luxor to the Valley of the Kings, the only transport was by donkey!

At last in November 1922 the great moment arrived. The steps were revealed for a second time and, at the bottom, was a plastered-up door. Carter removed a corner and shone in a candle but all he could see was a tunnel filled with rubble put there by the priest to deter further robbers. It took another two days to clear a passageway to a second door. Again a corner was removed and Carter stepped forward with a candle. There was a stunned silence from Carter before Carnarvon very nervously said: "Can you see anything?" "Yes," replied Carter. "Wonderful things."

LORD CARNARVON, EVELYN HERBERT, HOWARD CARTER
IN THE VALLEY OF THE KINGS

My mother was the first person to enter for 3,000 years. She was only 21. Carter enlarged the hole and helped her in with a torch. She remembered in particular the alabaster vases, the ebony figures and the large quantity of gold glittering in the torchlight. If she had been allowed to have just one item, she always said that she loved one of the smallest alabaster vases, which had a tiny lion carved on the top with its little pink tongue sticking out.

In the anteroom alone were 500 pieces, among them gilded animals, four chariots, two life-size guardian figures, carved chairs overlaid with gilt and gold everywhere. To make King Tutankhamun incorruptible after death, two tons of gold was employed in his burial. His gold portrait mask is without parallel as a masterpiece of ancient art.

Then began the colossal work of photographing, cataloguing and moving all the artefacts. In total, 5,000 items were removed from the tomb. First, everything had to be coated with wax to stop it crumbling on contact with the air. Altogether, the painstaking work took seven years to complete. When the excavation was finished, the young king's mummy was replaced in the tomb. Carnarvon had insisted on it, much to the annoyance of the museum authorities, and his wishes were carried out.

The tomb was divided into four chambers – the fourth containing the gold sarcophagus and the boy king's mummified body. Very sadly, Carnarvon, after all his years of toil and hope, never lived to see the final sarcophagus. Already exhausted by the work, he was bitten by a mosquito, he cut the bite while shaving and septicaemia developed. Within four days he was dead. Had penicillin existed, he would no doubt have survived.

My mother was with him, and his wife very bravely flew out to Egypt in a single-engine plane but his son, who was serving in India, arrived too late. The British Army was then in charge of the services in Cairo. At the precise time of

Carnarvon's death, all the lights in the city went out for no apparent technical reason. The chief Royal Engineer in charge of services in the city reported that no fault could be found but 20 minutes later, the lights came on again all over Cairo.

At the same time at Highclere, Carnarvon's Jack Russell terrier Susie was sleeping in the housekeeper's room. At the precise moment of her master's death, she sat up in her basket, howled and dropped down dead.

Another strange co-incidence was that the young boy king's mummy had a scar on his face at exactly the same place that the mosquito had bitten Carnarvon's face. Lord Carnarvon's death and the strange tales surrounding it, resurrected the legend of the Curse of the Kings.

This would originally have been a story put about at the time of the burial to deter the tomb robbers. Nevertheless, King Tutankhamun's tomb had been raided shortly after his death, but the culprits must have been disturbed and, apart from breaking pieces of gold from the chariot wheels, they mostly made off with unguents, scents and ointments which, in those days, were of great value. One of the unguents in the jars still bore the imprint of a robber's finger. The tomb had been left in a terrible mess, with everything turned over in piles and disturbed, just as your house might look if it had been burgled.

The Queen opened the exhibition at the British Museum and we had a wonderful tour with the head of the Egyptology department, Professor Edwards. He gave us a detailed description of the king's short life – the games he played, his hunting, his beliefs and his great love for his young wife.

When the coffin was opened, a very small wreath was found placed on the king's chest. In the coffin were two pathetic embalmed foetuses – it is thought his wife never produced live progeny. He came to the throne at the age of nine and died at nineteen.

The previous king had insisted his people should worship one god, Aten, a relatively minor aspect of the sun god. This was very unpopular, causing riots and trouble throughout the country. However, the young king set about reverting to the previous religion and restoring the cults of the old gods. He had a very difficult reign and, during the nine years he was on the throne, made many enemies. It was therefore thought that he had probably been murdered, until recently, when his mummy was put through an MRI scanner and it was discovered that he had a very bad break to his leg, which had never healed. It is most likely that he died of septicaemia following an accident.

While I was in Egypt, the pilots of the Egyptian Air Lines, our hotel manager, guides and a museum official all shook my hand and thanked me for what the family had done for the country. In the USA alone, seven million people visited the Tutankhamun exhibition. In London, queues formed right around the British Museum and it was the same story in Paris. The find fired the imagination of the world.

The prime movers in organising the first exhibition were the French and, under the direction of Madame Bettencourt, the head of the French Egyptology department, all the treasures were beautifully and precisely restored, having deteriorated considerably in the Cairo Museum.

The reason gold was so valuable and revered was that it was not indigenous to Egypt and had to be brought into the country from other parts of Africa. King Tutankhamun's tomb is probably one of the least rich among the tombs because he died so young. Pharaohs spent their lifetimes amassing objects of great value and beauty to be buried with them when they died. A boy of 19 would not have had much time to prepare and embellish his tomb, nor to collect great treasures.

The Egyptians believed that they had to go across the River Styx to reach the other world, so they were buried with their boats, their ebony carved slaves and the food to sustain them during the journey. Their picnic baskets! Some of the wheat seeds and food were still preserved there and I believe wheat has actually been grown from the ancient seed.

Apart from all the work of the excavation, enormous pressure was put upon Carnarvon and Carter by the world's press. Carnarvon decided to give sole rights to The Times, with permission for that paper to handle the world's requests for news, intending to deflect the attention and distraction away from the archaeologists. But this turned out to be a grave mistake and only intensified the difficulties and problems – especially from the Egyptian papers. Tourists visiting the adjacent tomb of Rameses were also a nightmare.

The Metropolitan Museum in New York was immensely helpful, sending a team of experts to help with all the work and cataloguing. The head of the Museum lived in a large house in New York City, which changed hands many times over the years until, in the 1970s, it was left to a family with young boys.

One day a visitor saw a go-cart in the garage with a set of very strange silver wheels. The boy's go-cart tyres had punctured and, while exploring the attic, he had found these round tins, very suitable for wheel replacements. These turned out to be the tins containing the original film of the opening of the tomb, as shot by Carnarvon himself! Old films can explode and are supposed to be treated with respect but these were perfectly preserved, despite their experiences.

In the end, nothing from the tomb went to the Carnarvon or Carter families. When a concession to dig was granted, a clause of the contract said that the discoverer could share 50 per cent of everything – apart from the mummies and sarcophagi. But a new Frenchman had just been appointed head of the Antiquity Department and he wished to keep all the treasures for the Egyptian Museum.

He managed to find a line qualifying that the sharing clause only referred to tombs that were non-entire – probably because it was not envisaged that an entire tomb would ever be discovered. This upset Carnarvon, as he wished some of the treasures to go to the British Museum.

Had he lived to negotiate the point, the result might have been different but Carter was notoriously aggressive in his manner and did not have a gift for negotiation.

There have been stories that Carnarvon and Carter stole some items from the tomb but these are totally incorrect. For one thing, there would have been no point, as they still anticipated that 50 per cent of the find was theirs by right. Carnarvon was always accompanied on his expeditions by his daughter Evelyn, my mother. This was because his wife was disinterested in Egyptology, hated the life in Egypt and found the prevalent cobras an abomination.

Carnarvon wished to be buried on his estate at the top of Beacon Hill, overlooking his land and his beloved stud farm. When driving along the Newbury-Winchester Road, the fence surrounding the grave on the top of the hill can just be seen. Originally, the grave was just an area of grass surrounded by a wire fence. However, when Beacon Hill was designated a beauty spot and visited by the public, there was nothing to show that it was not a huge waste paper basket, so my mother decided that a stone should be erected on his grave.

The day came for the Service of Consecration for the stone, which was to be performed by the Bishop. He gave a very good service but, at the end of it, he turned to my mother and said, "Tell me, Lady Evelyn, where is your father buried?"

When we all returned to the Castle for lunch, the Bishop said to his wife, "I am sure you would like to go and wash." She looked surprised, but duly left the room. The Bishop turned to his host and said: "I am so appalled by my terrible mistake. Please may I have a double vodka." It is pleasing to note that even Bishops are human!

My mother was so traumatised by her father's death that she never went back to Egypt. As a result, she had never seen the sarcophagus or the amazing golden mask until the opening of the exhibition at the British Museum.

At the time of the Exhibition, the television people and journalists kept ringing up and asking her to talk about the curse but she herself did not believe it. She told them simply that she was alive and kicking at 71.

When she had gone on her honeymoon to New York, the quayside was packed with reporters, not interested in the discovery at all but shouting: "Hi, Mam. Tell us how King Tut killed your Pa."

In 2009 there is a new Tutankhamun exhibition at Highclere Castle set up by the present Lord and Lady Carnarvon which is well worth viewing.

★ ★ ★

One of Simon's hobbies was buying old motor wrecks and putting them back together. When he came back from Australia, he bought himself a Piper. It was so low to the ground, I was unable to go in it more than once as it had grounded on a cat's eye! The roof tended to leak, much to the dismay of his fiancée, Cristina, who sat in a permanent puddle! The car was made of fibreglass, went extremely fast and I'm sure was horribly dangerous. In fact, the man who invented and manufactured them in Wokingham, died in a crash at the wheel of his Piper.

One of Simon's friends once left the house without his mackintosh and, when Simon found it, he jumped into the car and drove after him. The weather was fairly wet and, the next thing he knew, he was skidding across someone's garden, having knocked their fence down and mashed up their roses. The lady who owned the house was absolutely furious, shouting at him for being such a bad driver. Simon had no idea whose garden he was in until one of his friends came to the door and started to shout, "Mummy, stop. It's Simon", whereupon the mother replied: "I don't care who he is, no-one should be driving like that."

Simon had no idea what he wanted to do when he left school and vacillated from helicopter pilot to schoolteacher. One day we were having dinner with a great friend Rennie Maudslay, who had in fact been a pageboy for my mother and father when they married. During dinner, we discussed Simon's prospects and he said it was his belief that the best career was accountancy. It didn't necessarily mean you would go on to be an accountant but it could give a good grounding and be a jumping off point for many different things.

However, as one friend of Simon's put it, he himself never managed to jump! Simon did exceptionally well in his exams and was eventually posted to Brussels.

Both our sons married quite young. It was amazing that Simon's romance with his wife ever got off the ground. He sat next to a very pretty girl at a party and asked her if she would like to go out for dinner the following week. She accepted and gave him her address. But when he went round there and rang the doorbell, the first thing he said was; "Does Cristiana live here?" She said: "Yes – that's me." He had failed to recognise her after a week. They eventually got married, have been very happy and have two splendid sons.

They married in Germany and Michael and I decided to motor across. As it was a fairly hot day, we had the roof of the Mercedes down. We were driving through a small town when suddenly, my hat, which was sitting on the back seat of the car, blew away and, before we could rescue it, was run over by a bus. Sadly, when we got to church, the bridegroom's mother looked anything but immaculate!

It was a very good service and afterwards, Dr and Mrs Stein, Cristiana's parents, gave an excellent dinner party for all their friends and relations, as well as a number of Simon's friends, who had also come over. Michael, whose mother had sent him out to Germany to learn the language as soon as he left school, made a speech in the best German he could muster after so many years. I'm not at all sure he was very good, but everyone was extremely polite about it. We had a great time and couldn't have got on any more splendidly with Cristiana's parents.

Their first son, Antony, was born in London. Both Simon and Cristiana enjoyed Simon's posting in Brussels and Cristiana's fluency in French was helpful to them.

When they came back to this country, Simon worked in London and they found a very nice house adjacent to Hyde Park. They were living there when their second son Nicholas was born.

They were very fortunate that they were able to have children. They went to Brazil on honeymoon and, on their return, Cristiana was very ill. The doctor said it was glandular fever and not to give her antibiotics. But she was deteriorating so fast that I took the decision to ring another doctor I knew in New York, who specialised in tropical diseases. I told him the symptoms and he said it seemed to him that it was a case of typhoid. He referred her to a specialist who diagnosed that it was indeed typhoid and she was immediately admitted to hospital, where they managed to save her life, but said it was likely that she would never be able to have children.

As the boys grew up, they decided it would be nicer for them to live in the country and they bought a lovely converted orangery in Berkshire. It was an interesting house, all on the ground floor, and the walls at either end of the long room were cavities in which hay or straw would originally have been packed to keep it warm in the winter. The orangery part of the building was of a considerable age and the house to which it had belonged was Georgian. A large red brick wall surrounded the garden.

One of Simon's friends from Eton came from Eastern Asia and used to visit them at weekends. On one occasion, his father paid a visit and Simon was showing him the garden. In the brick wall were a number of holes and, when he saw them, he said: "I suppose these bullet holes were made when you shot people?" Simon was horrified and had to explain that they were where they fixed the wires up which the trees were trained.

Antony and Nicholas followed their father to Eton and both were wet bobs. They went on to University, where they did extremely well and both have excellent jobs in London.

Simon is now a hard working financial advisor to a number of companies but, whenever possible, he and Cristiana come down to see me, bringing lots of delicacies, smoked salmon and a wonderful arrangement of flowers, which lasts for weeks.

While Edward was at prep school, he became so severely ill that it was considered likely he was suffering from leukaemia. Only after endless tests and visits to hospital, which he loathed, did it turn out to be an extremely bad case of glandular fever. The illness took a real hold. It had started at school and he continued to play games, unaware of the fact that the best thing for glandular fever is to be kept still and get plenty of rest. On one occasion at school, he felt so unwell during games that he threw himself to the ground in the middle of a race and got into trouble with the master, who criticised him for chickening out of the race because he thought he could not win it. When he was eventually diagnosed we were told that he must be kept really quiet – but how on earth do you subdue a 12-year-old who is simply mad about games?

One day I was playing bridge at Crockfords and there was a charming young man there of about 35. I asked him what he did for a living and he replied: "I teach bridge." I told him I had a son who loved card games and asked if he would mind giving him lessons twice a week. It turned out to be one of the best things I ever did. Edward took to it like a duck to water, loved every minute of it and has never looked back. He is now a very fine county player.

It took about eight years for him to recover completely and, even now, he tends to get tired. On leaving school, Edward decided to spend his Gap year in Africa, working for Anglo-American and staying with friends, and he loved it. On his weekends off, he used to go to Madagascar, which he thought was the most wonderful place on earth, with its unbelievably beautiful birds and animals.

While he was in Africa, he earned and saved quite a lot of money, so on his return, he was able to buy himself a Datsun motorcar. He went to work for Rothschilds, who thought very highly of him and, in fact, he was soon doing the same work as people who had been there for five years, and was really enjoying it.

That was until one night he went out to dinner with friends in London. He was quite sober as he never drank but, on his way home, it was raining slightly. As he was driving along Knightsbridge, someone stepped off the pavement in front of him. He braked, but his car skidded and overturned into the underpass. It took the emergency services two hours to cut him out and he said the worst thing about it was that the whole time the car stereo kept repeating the same tune over and over again.

Luckily it was a Japanese car as they were reinforced with side supports. They saved his life but, even so, there were only six inches left between the roof and the floor. He was taken to St George's Hospital where it was discovered that he had bruised his brain and the doctors advised that he shouldn't work for a year. Rothschilds very generously offered to pay his salary for 12 months, even though it was not certain that he would be well enough to go back to work at the end of the year. As it happened, he was not sufficiently recovered to go back to a full-time job but his father refused to allow the bank to pay him.

Edward went to his cousin Jane Hanbury's 21st birthday party, and from across the room he saw a girl called Scarlet Hardwick who he rather liked the look of. He asked her out to dinner and that night, he told his flatmate: "I have just seen the girl I'm going to marry." It took him some months to persuade Scarlet that he was right. Her family was very displeased because they felt she was too young and had only just left Heathfield. Until then, I never believed in love at first sight but they did indeed marry and have been very happy. She has been a wonderful wife to him and they have two lovely children – a boy and a girl, Eve and Alexander.

They were married in Wimbledon and Scarlet's parents gave them a super reception in the garden of their house. Many of Edward's friends came, as well as both sets of relations, and it was a great party. There was just one small drama. In the garden, they had a large fish pond, which was covered with a rather pretty green plant. My Norwich terrier took this to be grass and stepped straight into the pond, whereupon she sank – glug, glug, glug – straight to the bottom. For what seemed like an eternity, she remained out of sight and I thought she had got stuck in the mud. I was screaming for help until, in a moment, she rose to the surface, bubbling up with a most surprised expression on her face.

After the bride and bridegroom had left, our hosts gave a very good dinner party for friends and family, at which we met the various relations.

Simon and Cristiana were staying the night with us and at around ten o' clock we set off for home in our different cars. In Chobham, we drove past the scene of an accident, with a number of people and police standing about. We didn't think anything of it until we got home. The telephone was ringing. It was Cristiana sobbing that Simon had killed somebody and please would we come back at once.

We drove back and it transpired that a girl coming out of pub had fallen into the road in front of the car. Cristiana jumped out and said to the boy who was with her, "you pushed her", whereupon he got hold of Cristiana by the throat and started shaking her.

Fortunately, several witnesses confirmed that he had indeed pushed the girl into the road and the publican said that the two had been drinking and fighting all night. It was obvious that Simon had been at a wedding, so he was breathalysed but found to be below the limit. Then, when the ambulance arrived, the girl turned out not to be dead – just dead drunk! Eventually the police told him they were sorry he had had such an unpleasant experience on his brother's wedding day and sent him home in the clear.

Edward and Scarlet went to live in Ireland and bought a lovely Georgian house in Galway which they turned into a small hotel.

EDWARD AND SCARLET WITH THEIR FIRST CHILD, EVELYN,
AND BLAZER LOOKING VERY DISAPPROVING.

Among other things, they hosted the hunt ball for the Galway Blazers. We used to go over there and stay and had some marvellous times. Scarlet is an excellent cook, so we always had the most superb food.

It was amazing in Ireland. If one ever stopped to ask someone the way, they would take a full five minutes to tell you, only to add with a smile, "But I wouldn't start from here, if I were you."

After we left the pig farm, we went to live in London again because my mother had had a series of strokes and my father was also ill, so we wanted to be near them. We were soon bored doing nothing and, when we were asked if we would like to run King Fahad's son's London office, we were willing to give it a try.

If Arabs find you reliable and honest with one task, they soon want to do everything through you until, in the end, we were sending frozen chickens, medical supplies and sporting goods to the value of £250,000 to Saudi Arabia every month. Lilywhites were wonderfully helpful, managing to supply us with all the sports equipment that was required.

There was one man in Dohar in Qatar who owned a huge palace but chose to sleep in a tent in the garden because he said he found it more agreeable. One day, one of my friends said to me, "I would like to take you out to see our brand new dual carriageway. We got into the car and sped down the new road like an arrow until, after a few miles, he suddenly slammed on the brakes. The road finished there and straight ahead there was nothing but desert! Still it was a way of life that I very much enjoyed.

We lived in a garden flat in Eaton Square, which we chose because of our Labradors and because Michael liked gardening. But reaching the flat entailed going down in a lift, rather than up and therefore lost us a lot of kudos with several of our friends because Arabs think it's only worthwhile to live in a penthouse and to go downwards to one's living quarters is definitely something shameful.

While we were working in London, we were introduced to an engineer in Kent, who had invented a very special form of bullet-proof concrete, for use in building.

The manner of manufacturing houses from this concrete could not have been simpler. A large steel mould was laid down into which were placed the windows, doors, electrical wiring and pipes for the plumbing. Then a machine, which the same man had also invented and developed, travelled the length of the mould, adding the concrete. This particular concrete, known as slabcon, dried very hard, so that a whole wall could be lifted out of the mould with all the fittings already in place. We ended up sending a number of units out to Saudi Arabia and I think they were erected in Jedda.

Not only was the concrete bullet proof but it also insulated very well against heat. On the whole though, I thought they were less than suitable for the Arab market as they like their ceilings very high. But if slabcon walls were made high enough for their tastes, they became too heavy to transport.

A number of houses were built out of it for the MoD, including a whole village modelled to look like a typical Irish town, in which soldiers who were going over to Ireland could train with live ammunition.

It was vital training, as they had to be aware that a terrorist may be hiding behind any wall but, equally, the next person to emerge into their line of vision might be a child. Only realistic training could teach them how to respond quickly but not indiscriminately.

During this time, we took on an excellent managing director called Mr Perrior. We were approached by the French government and asked to build houses for a nudist colony or, as it was politely termed, a naturist reserve. Mr Perrior was invited down to Kent to give a talk about the houses. He told me afterwards that he had been rather horrified because, when he arrived at the meeting, nobody there had any clothes on. I said to him, "Whatever did you do?" and he replied, "I loosened my tie."

He travelled to a number of places in Europe, including Germany, where they are very keen on naturism, but unfortunately the finance was not forthcoming and we eventually had to discontinue the project.

Soon after that, I was invited by Saga to start giving lectures about Tutankhamun. I would go every Sunday to Highclere Castle to talk to the people who visited on the Saga buses and, eventually, they extended an invitation to go to Egypt and lecture on the cruise boats going up the Nile. I jumped at the opportunity because I had never been to Egypt myself and nor had my mother been back there since her father's death.

My visit took place very shortly after the massacre of tourists in the Valley of the Kings. Some people had managed to escape with their lives by crawling under their tour bus, so I said to my son Edward, don't worry about me while I'm gone. If anything happens, I shall hide under the bus. I am a large woman and he simply looked at me in utter amazement and said: "But Mum, you'll never fit under a bus. They'll have to jack it up first!" I thought that was a really funny remark.

When you go on these PR trips, you have to sit through endless dinners. One night we were having dinner in Cairo with some Lebanese and the conversation had rather faded out, so I produced my funny story. The room fell into absolute silence and one of our hosts looked at me said: "Those were our clients." I wished the floor to open up and swallow me but, unfortunately, it didn't.

I loved Egypt, however. Sailing down the Nile and watching people living their lives as they must have done since time immemorial – doing their washing in the river with their donkeys standing by – was fascinating.

We went to Egypt in May, which was not an ideal time to go, as it was extremely hot. When we came to Tutankhamun's tomb, there was a steep slope down into it and I could see that fairly young people were coming back up panting for breath. As I was just recuperating following my motor accident and stroke, and not wishing to see the headline 'King Tut strikes again', I decided not to attempt it. I was rather annoyed some time later when I read in Saga's magazine that I had refused to go down for fear of Tutankhamun's curse. While I was waiting outside the tomb, there was a party of English tourists and a party of Japanese. When their guides told them I was the granddaughter of the man who discovered the tomb the Japanese were so excited and all clustered round bowing and shaking my hand, while the English remained quite unmoved.

While we were in Egypt, wherever our coach went, it was escorted by the local police. We were travelling on a major road when, suddenly, the police car in front jumped on its brakes and we very nearly ran into the back of it. We all fell off our seats, convinced that we had come under terrorist attack, but the cause turned out to be a donkey and cart, which was going the wrong way down the dual carriageway.

My father had died in 1976 and my mother in 1980, so we decided to return to the country. We bought, Kingsmoor, a very large house on Sunningdale golf course, which had the most beautiful garden. The property had at one time belonged to the owners of Waterers, the garden centre. It was extremely large, with 14 bedrooms, so we divided half of it into a house for Edward and Scarlet, who had returned from Ireland when the Bobby Sands hunger strike and several other troubles meant it was no longer thought to be safe for English people to remain there.

THE GARDEN AT KINGSMOOR

When we moved in, we were surprised to find that none of the downstairs windows had any curtains. It transpired that the house had previously belonged to an American who was a tremendous snob and, upon her death, had left the house to the most elevated person she could find, in the shape of Lady Mary Burley. The reason there were no curtains was that the American lady had left in her will a stipulation that the curtains on the ground floor should never be drawn, as she wished to be able to look in and enjoy the parties!

When eventually Edward and Scarlet decided to move out into a home of their own at Englefield Green, we broke the house up into retirement flats. We had some marvellous residents there, with whom we became very friendly. We used to run a sort of 'evening social session' before dinner every night.

One of the residents, whose wife had died, kept her ashes in an urn on the mantelpiece in his room. The reason for this was quite practical – he and his wife had wanted to be buried together but there was a rule on her family estate that only people born there could be buried there. Because of that, the only way that they could be together in death was by amalgamating her ashes with his at the time of his death.

At the time, we had a first rate, but very superstitious, Irish cook. She used to take him his hot milk in a thermos to have at his bedside at night until one day she came back down the stairs screaming "The ashes have exploded! The ashes have exploded!" We couldn't believe our ears and went to investigate the situation, only to discover that the bang that had so terrified her was in fact caused by the steam from the milk blowing the top off the thermos. But despite endless reassurance, she would never go in that room again.

We had a property company but, by 1985, we felt the property market was overheating and office space was becoming increasingly difficult to let, so we diverted our attention to the care home market, as we were advised that there was always a ready demand. Our first venture was to buy a 56-bed nursing home in Ilfracombe, where we had a very efficient matron.

It was around that time, while I was travelling up and down to Devon, that I started to find that I was falling asleep on the motorway and having to pull over to the side. It turned out that I was in fact diabetic but had not previously been diagnosed. The doctor recommended that I take a rest and hand over to my business partner, whose wife was a state registered nurse.

Suddenly, to our absolute horror, Michael and I received a letter from the bank, foreclosing and demanding payment of two million pounds. Our partner, it transpired, had not been paying the mortgage in my absence - nor even the staff's wages or matron's maternity pay. He promptly disappeared without a trace and, to this day, has never reappeared. This was a terrible blow and it took a long time to recover, but in the end, we had built up several homes, both nursing and residential. The work entailed lots of travelling because, instead of buying homes adjacent to where we lived, our principle was to go wherever the best homes were, which meant travelling as far north as Yorkshire.

We got to know some delightful people and the work we all did was well worthwhile. We really enjoyed the work and loved making sure that the residents were happy and well fed and that the homes were clean and didn't smell. It's amazing how many otherwise good homes do smell but when you mention it to the matron, she will say, "Does it really?" because, of course, the staff get used to it.

One day, a woman came to one of our homes to see her old friend and said to her, "Do you know who I am?" The friend replied, "No, but if you ask at reception, they'll tell you." One old lady who always used to have a dog was in the habit of asking: "Where's my dog? The staff didn't want to make her unhappy by telling her he had died, so they would tell her he was sleeping upstairs and she would be happy for the rest of the day. On one occasion, an old man was sitting on the sofa with her. When she asked after the dog and received the usual reply, he turned to her and said: "Yes that damn dog barked all night and kept me awake!"

One Home had an annexe to the main house for two people and you had to go outside in order to reach it. Although we were in a small town and the annexe was situated at the back of the house, this inspector eventually demanded that we build a glass walkway between the two parts of the house to prevent muggings – something that had not happened in that location for 27 years. The cost of the work would be £22,000. We appealed, but to no avail. A small home for 14 people just couldn't run to that kind of expense, so, in the end, we had to close it.

I found a nice place in a home that was expanding, where six of the residents could go together and some of our staff went there too. But you can't move people of 90 who are happy without consequences and, within six months, I heard that only one was still alive. One lady wanted to join her daughter and live with her but social services objected, saying that the lady could not live abroad. 'Abroad' turned out to be Wales!

It was during the time that we were acquiring and running nursing homes that Michael became ill. He suffered for five years, having to be constantly rushed off to hospital. For a long time, the doctors failed to establish a cause. To this day it has not been diagnosed with any certainty but it has been put down to a one-in-a-million allergy to a gout medication. He had always been a martyr to gout, which is an agonising condition. He very seldom drank port, to which gout is often wrongly attributed, but his doctors told us that eating offal such as liver and kidneys and any kind of shellfish was equally inadvisable.

On one occasion he had been rushed to the Royal Berkshire Hospital at Reading but the conditions and over-crowding there were so terrible that I stepped in and managed to get him transferred to Kind Edward VII Hospital for Officers in London. We called in the top specialists and were confident that he would recover. But one night, very suddenly, his heart gave out. I received the call at about 5am and alerted the boys but by the time we got to London, it was too late.

After Michael died, I rented a lovely flat in a block overlooking an attractive courtyard garden with fountains. But, after a few weeks, strange things started to happen. First a chair often seemed to be in a different position in the morning to where it had been left the night before. Then, on going into the lounge one morning, a mackintosh, which had been on a hook, was laid out on the floor, as though for a picnic. Then the cleaner came in one day with a jar of mayonnaise asking if I had meant to throw it away, because she had found it in the dog's drinking bowl. Soon, at night, someone began knocking gently on the door, rather tentatively, like a child visiting the headmaster. It gradually progressed to the door opening nine inches or so and then closing again. It happened several times a night, which caused my dog to go ballistic.

It was becoming quite frightening, so I contacted the local clergyman and asked if he could perform an exorcism service. He called to see me but explained that it would be three or four weeks before the exorcism could be carried out, as the Church of England had quite a waiting list. Shortly afterwards, I saw in the local paper that there was a medium coming to give a lecture in the town, so I telephoned him and asked him if he could deal with ghosts. He said yes, he certainly could, so I asked him to visit me. He arrived in a large car with blacked out windows. He proved to be a charming man. He had been a fireman and one of his young colleagues had died. After that, he kept hearing the young man's voice in his head, telling him that he would be able to help people if only he would take his gift seriously. Quickly he found that he was so successful and so busy that he had to give up his life as a fireman and become a full-time medium. He explained to me that he would take the ghost away with him and show it the light. Ghosts, he said, are usually just people who have missed the light, which was only visible for a short time. He said that my flat was inhabited by a young boy, who was really just enjoying himself. I felt rather mean moving him on but my fireman friend assured me that he would be perfectly happy to go.

While he was there, the medium asked to look around the rest of the house. There was a communal dining room, which they could never get warm, however many radiators they employed. He said that there was an old man living in the dining room, who had been there a very long time and that he would take him along too. From that moment on, the dining room was as warm as toast and never needed heating. It really was an amazing experience that I shall never forget.

SIMON

My family has always seemed to have an unusual number of psychic experiences. I believe that Simon is psychic in a completely different way. He never gambles but sometimes he would come to the casino with us and he could walk up to the roulette table and say "17", whereupon it would immediately come up. "32", "20" – he could always do it three or four times before saying: "That's it. I'm exhausted."

Once, when I was young, I went to a dance at a friend's house. They had a beautiful garden and it was a lovely summer's evening, so another friend and I went for a walk between two herbaceous borders, backed by yew hedges. As we were returning to the party, a woman walked by. We looked at each other and said, who was that, because we had thought we knew everyone at the party. But, when we looked again, the woman had disappeared. She couldn't have gone anywhere, because we were completely enclosed by yew hedges. There is a theory that many people see ghosts but don't realise what has happened. In retrospect, I certainly believe that was one of those occasions. After my experience with the haunted flat, the people who had bought Garden House from us very kindly offered me a flat in our old annexe, to which I returned on my own.

I sold most of the nursing homes and became a consultant. I looked at about 50 homes a year, from Scotland to the Isle of Man but probably only ten per cent of them were worth seeing twice.

I was happy living in the annexe and was directly adjacent to the golf course, where I still played each day. Things were going well until, one day, I was turning into my gate when the woman driving the car behind failed to notice and ploughed straight into the side of me. There was an enormous bang but, thankfully, the car didn't turn over. I was confident at the moment of my accident that I had escaped unhurt. But in fact, the impact had torn the arteries in my neck. Two weeks later, I suffered a stroke. It was very lucky when the stroke happened I was off to London to play bridge. I was on my way out when I thought I had better let the dog out first. I fell flat on my face outside but it was indeed fortunate that I was still at home as, moments later, I would have been driving on the M4 and would no doubt have caused a terrible accident.

I was in hospital for a month before I returned, hoping to resume my old life. But one major thing had changed. I had completely lost my balance and found it impossible to play golf. It all became too much and I moved out of the annexe into Dormy House nursing home in Sunningdale. I was still living directly opposite the golf club and continued to see all my friends and go round the course on a golf buggy while Edward and my grandsons were playing.

At that time, my daughter-in-law Scarlet had been bequeathed a very lovely old house in Chilmark in Wiltshire, which had belonged to her grandparents and then to her aunt. The house was supposed to be haunted by the ghost of a little girl, who walked the stairs. But none of the family ever saw her apart from Edward, who has definitely inherited some psychic ability from my mother. The only other person to see the little girl was the telephone engineer who installed their telephones. The house was empty and he was so terrified by the experience that he ran away, leaving all his equipment behind him.

Parts of the house were very old indeed and some of the stone walls were two feet thick. It was very unusual and extremely attractive to dine in the dining room as it had no electricity and was warmed by a large log fire and lit by a candelabra bristling with dozens of candles.

I remained at Dormy House for some time until Edward suggested that I come down and live near them. I found a lovely flat but it offered no regular care, just Warden supervision. Edward asked whether, after my years in nursing homes, I would be able to manage on my own. I said yes, of course I would, but it turned out that he was so right and I had to move on.

I moved into the BUPA nursing home where I still live and of which I cannot speak too highly. I was even allowed to bring my little dog Mitzie, who was originally a rescue dog and belonged to the lady in the room next to mine at Dormy House.

Mitzie had previously spent four years with a man, who bought her as a puppy, but had to go into hospital and could no longer look after her. She went into Battersea Dogs' Home and, from there, to an old lady of 83. When she became ill and had to move into a nursing home, the dog was also made very welcome. Mitzie was allowed in the lounge until, one day, she escaped and was eventually found queuing for sausages at the local Waitrose. The next time was not so funny – she had strayed onto the electric railway line. After that, she was shut in her owner's bedroom all day and sometimes, for a change, I would have her in my room. She was always an amazingly caring little dog. Her mistress used to fall down at night and be unable to reach the bell to raise the alarm. But whenever it happened, Mitzie would bark in a certain way, which I came to recognise, so that I could ring the bell and fetch the carer, who lived at the other end of the building.

One day, Mitzie's owner said to the carer: "I want to go and see Mrs Leatham." She was told no, and that I was too busy, although, in fact, I think the carer just didn't want the long walk.   Fortunately, the old lady insisted and, in the end, she got her way. She came in but all she said to me was: "I just wanted to thank you for looking after my little dog". That very same night she died and it seemed to me that what she really meant to say was please will you look after my little dog when I am gone?

She was found at 6.30 in the morning, with Mitzie clinging to her, shaking all over and in a very traumatised state. I believe the old lady must have died at about 4am because, every night at that time, she will come around and nuzzle me to make sure that I am OK. She is still very insecure.

I had actually already had a timeshare dog, Dena. I shared her with Freda, a friend of mine in Sunningdale – she had her during the week when I was busy and I had her at the weekends when my friend was busy. She was a beautiful little Norwich Terrier. When I went to live in Dorset, she started spending all the time with Freda, who absolutely adored her. Unfortunately, after five years, Dena became ill. She had a heart attack and was rushed to the vet, who managed to resuscitate her with oxygen but decided that she ought to go straight to hospital. Freda dashed up with Dena's favourite toy, so that she could have it in hospital with her. But, as she arrived, the dog had a relapse and died in Freda's arms. I'm not sure she will ever get over it. Dena was such a very special little dog and meant so much to her. She was cremated and lies in a lovely casket in the garden, with pansies flowering all around the spot.

It is a real joy to be here. I see a lot of Edward and, while I have excellent care, I am able to retain my free time, which allows me to play plenty of bridge.

I took up bridge in earnest after Michael died. Initially, I played off and on with friends in London clubs and now I play more and more, as there are some very good bridge clubs nearby. Sometimes I play with Edward, but he is such a very good player that, if I'm playing a hand rather badly, he will look at me and say, "Oh, Mum", in such a depressed voice that I try to find other partners, as it doesn't seem right to depress him!

All my life, I have been very lucky to have marvellous friends – school friends, Wren friends, golfing friends and social friends too numerous to name. But there were three very special friends, all of whom have now left us. Sarah Beckwith-Smith was a tremendous friend to both Michael and me. She was wonderfully amusing, with a bubbly personality. Her father had died in a Japanese prisoner of war camp and she had two brothers and a sister. Her mother was a charming person, who had a lovely old house in Berkshire, as well as a large estate in Scotland where I used to go and spend August. The first time I stayed with them, I drove up with a friend, an enterprise which made my mother very anxious as I had only just passed my driving test and had never driven any distance before. Fortunately, in those days, there was not nearly so much traffic on the roads and the journey passed off quite quietly.

Sarah married Johnny Henderson, who had been Monty's ADC, and they lived in a lovely old house near

Newbury. We used to stay with each other a lot. She had a daughter and two sons, one of whom is Nicky Henderson, the famous National Hunt trainer. One Tuesday, I spoke to her and she said to me: "Nicky is riding at Newbury on Saturday and I do wish he wouldn't because I feel sure something terrible is going to happen." Before the week was out, she had died, leaving a husband and three children.

She was a first class rider, Master of the Craven Hunt, and she was out hunting when her horse shied and she was thrown off. Her hat rolled off and the horse kicked her head in. It was a terrible tragedy, as she was such a wonderful person. Her Memorial Service was held at St Margaret's, Westminster, and there were so many people there that some of them had to stand at the back of the church. Sadly, her brothers and sisters have all since died. Rather extraordinarily, her sister died in a motor accident many years later but on the same date that Sarah was killed.

Another great friend of mine was Diana Cunliffe-Owen. Her parents, Helen and Sir Hugo, had a beautiful house in Sunningdale with a lovely garden and a swimming pool and were good friends with my parents. They kept a number of Great Dane dogs and Helen could never go swimming without first shutting the dogs in because if one of them glimpsed her in the water they would jump in, thinking she was drowning, and pull her out. Nothing was safe from the dogs – they had even learned how to open doors. Helen used to go racing with my mother and Catherine, my aunt, and the Cunliffe-Owens would often stay at Highclere.

Helen was a medium – although she never practised. However, two or three times a year she would quite unexpectedly receive a message from above – she thought from her mother – tipping a horse that was certain to win. The messages would take unusual forms such as: "If you count the number of steps on that stand, it will equal the number of the horse that will win the next race." She was always right and people got to hear of it and would come up to her and ask if her mother had any tips. Once they were all at Highclere, practising on the Ouija board, when it spelled out the message: "Do not let him fly." The only person they knew who was likely to be flying in the near future was the fiancé of a girl who was part of the house party, who was a pilot. She telephoned him and managed to persuade him to cancel his next flight. The plane crashed and his co-pilot was killed.

Helen had two boys and two girls but she died when the children were very young and Sir Hugo asked my mother if she would mind keeping an eye on them. They had a very good nanny but we would go down to Sunningdale every weekend to spend time with them.

Eventually, Sir Hugo remarried a most unpleasant woman who sent them to school in sacks with holes cut in for the arms, while she used their clothes coupons for herself. My mother tried to help but found that interfering only made things worse and, sadly, in the end we didn't see them for a number of years. The eldest boy joined the fleet air arm and was killed on duty.

I didn't see any of the family again until Diana and I met up one day in a jeweller's shop. I was looking around and she was buying an engagement ring. She married a Canadian but some time later she returned to live in England and, because we played golf at the same course, we became firm friends.

Altogether, she was married four times. She was an excellent golfer and won the Berkshire County Championship four times. Her name is engraved on the cup with four different surnames!

Although she was younger than me, we enjoyed all the same things – racing, golf, bridge and gossip! She would often ring me with the latest piece of hot news. She had two children but, because she ran away from her husband with someone else, she was never allowed to see them until they came of age. But when they did, their first thought was to rush and find their mother.

One day I was telephoned and told that she had collapsed after breakfast, while she was getting something out of her car. She was rushed to Stoke Mandeville. I rang there and asked to speak to her but was told that she couldn't speak to me because she was busy arguing with the consultant and demanding to go to King Edward VII Hospital. I heard that soon after, she had started to read the Financial Times when she slumped and died of a heart attack. It was a shock to everyone who knew her as she was always thought to be in the best of health. We all miss her terribly.

One of our bridge and golf set was a most charming woman called Mary Dugan-Chapman. She was married to a very brave Polish pilot and they had a house in Wilton Crescent. They had two daughters – one a successful businesswoman and the other more literary-minded. When her husband Charles came out of the RAF he became a partner in a plastics factory. His business partner met him in a pub and broke the news that the Company was going bankrupt and he was leaving. Charles and Mary took the decision to take over the business and they worked immensely hard not only to put it back on the map but take it right to the top of the tree. It was known as Stuart Plastics and still has a very large factory near Croydon. They eventually sold the business for a great deal of money and after that Charles spent most of his time playing golf and bridge. They had a house in Sunningdale with a marvellous garden. They were renowned for their hospitality, their excellent food and company and their parties. Mary also ran a bridge game every weekend to which we always looked forward.

One day, their gardener was short-handed and Edward went over to help out. He was very fond of Mary and tremendously keen on gardening. He was sweeping up some leaves, and a curious robin was sitting on his wheelbarrow, watching him. Suddenly, the robin flew off in an agitated manner and Edward looked around to see standing behind him a beautiful woman in an old-fashioned dress, who smiled at him. He started to talk to her but she simply walked away and vanished into thin air.

She was so beautiful, he wanted to see her again, so he used to talk aloud while he was gardening and, once or twice, she did come back. One day we were leaving the house after bridge and Edward said: "Look, there she is." I looked but, of course, I could see nothing.

I also used to see a lot of Mary at the bridge club in London until her health began to deteriorate rather rapidly. She developed a tumour on the brain and eventually lost her battle.

Friends tend to make an enormous difference throughout one's life and I am very grateful that I have been so lucky.

SIMON AND CRISTIANA
ON THEIR 25TH WEDDING ANNIVERSARY
WITH ANTONY AND NICHOLAS.

My sons gave me a lovely 80th birthday party at a pub with absolutely superb food. Knowing my predilection for profiteroles, they had organised to have a birthday cake in the form of a giant pyramid of dozens of profiteroles with sparklers stuck into them, which were all lit as it was brought to the table.

THE FAMILY AT MY 80TH BIRTHDAY PARTY.
BACK ROW: EVE, ALEXANDER, ANTONY, NICHOLAS
FRONT ROW: EDWARD, SCARLET, SIMON, CRISTIANA

★ ★ ★

This is the short story of a long life but I'm having a great time and I hope it continues to get even longer.